Pat O'Hara

OPEN DISSENT

Open Dissent

An Uncompromising View of the Financial Crisis

Mike Soden

BLACKHALL
Publishing

Published by Blackhall Publishing
Lonsdale House
Avoca Avenue
Blackrock
Co. Dublin
Ireland

e-mail: info@blackhallpublishing.com
www.blackhallpublishing.com

© Mike Soden, 2010

ISBN: 978-1-84218-212-3

A catalogue record for this book is available from the British Library.

All rights reserved. No part of this publication may be reproduced,
stored in a retrieval system or transmitted in any form or by any
means, electronic, mechanical, photocopying, recording or
otherwise, without the prior, written permission of the publisher.

This book is sold subject to the condition that it shall not, by way
of trade or otherwise, be lent, resold, hired out, or otherwise
circulated without the publisher's prior consent in any form of
binding or cover other than that in which it is published and
without a similar condition including this condition being
imposed on the subsequent purchaser.

Printed in Ireland by ColourBooks Ltd.

ABOUT THE AUTHOR

Mike Soden was born in Dublin in January 1947. He attended Willow Park School and Blackrock College. After graduating from UCD in 1968 with a B.Comm. degree, he emigrated to Canada where he worked for Shell Canada Ltd and Xerox. He returned to Ireland in 1973 where he was appointed a loan officer with the Industrial Credit Company.

Mike's international career in banking was launched when he became branch manager for Citibank NA in Cork in 1975. The next ten years saw him relocate to London, Oslo, New York and Toronto in a variety of different capacities for the bank, including as global head of derivatives in New York and head of Citicorp Investment Bank Canada. In 1985 he was headhunted to set up an international capital markets organisation in London for Security Pacific, one of the top five banks in the US at the time.

Mike retired in 1990 from Security Pacific and remained so until the end of 1994, when he was approached to build a wholesale banking operation for National Australia Bank in London. In 2000 Mike was appointed global head of retail banking for National Australia Bank, with responsibility for 40,000 employees in 7 different banks and retail divisions in Australia, New Zealand, the US, the UK, Scotland and Ireland.

In 2001 he was approached to return to Ireland to become chief executive of the Bank of Ireland Group. He retired from Bank of Ireland in 2004.

All royalties from this book will form the author's contribution to 1 in 1000 – Running for Cystic Fibrosis (http://runningforcf.ie), which mobilised 1,000 women to participate in the Flora Mini Marathon on 7 June 2010.

1 in 1000 raised over €200,000 for a cystic fibrosis isolation unit in Our Lady's Children's Hospital, Crumlin.

PREFACE

On Sunday, 3 January 2010 I was a guest on RTÉ's Marian Finucane Show. The country having just experienced the worst financial year since the formation of the state, the reverberations of which would be felt for decades to come, was the background to the programme. The next day I received a call from Blackhall Publishing enquiring as to the likelihood of me writing a book on the subject of the financial crisis that was afflicting Ireland and the rest of the world. As a result of various meetings, I have proceeded on the basis that the objective of this book is to crystallise what happened to cause the crisis, internationally and nationally, why it has had such a particular effect on Ireland, and how and when we might see ourselves out of this conundrum. While many of us are looking for retribution for what has happened, I feel it best to leave the name, blame and shame game to an official enquiry.

The challenge of putting pen to paper on a subject in which I had been immersed over a 35-year career in banking seemed too good to pass up. I have spent years deeply involved in the international capital markets in London, New York, Toronto and Melbourne and I have gained experience in most areas within the financial system, ranging from debt to equity, branch banking to derivatives and commercial banking to investment banking. Much has been written on both the global and Irish financial and economic crisis to date. The one thing I, as an experienced insider, can bring to the table is a clear understanding of what best practice is in managing large numbers of complex financial activities around the world, which involves knowledge and experience in governance and the control of risk.

From my time serving on boards in Ireland I see that there is a particular culture prevalent that leads to the suppression of different opinions; I call this silent dissent. This is a somewhat intangible element of the reasons for the harshness of the crisis here. Leadership and governance are wanting in all areas of Irish society, most particularly, as recent events have demonstrated, in our Government and our banks. These themes need to be addressed in the context of our recovery; a lot of what I have to say in this book relates to our recovery and the embracement of a new reality, or a 'new normal'. I bring my own experiences of working in international banking into the book, along with observations on banking in Ireland and its future. The measures and remedies I suggest are the result of keeping my mind open to the best opportunities for Irish banking and the Irish economy. This book discusses these ideas openly, keeping in mind that they may not perhaps be palatable to everyone.

*For Lou, the most selfless and
dedicated partner one could have*

ACKNOWLEDGEMENTS

Beginning at the beginning, I thank Marian Finucane for having me on her show on 3 January 2010, an event from which the idea for this book was born. I appreciate Blackhall Publishing's initial interest in me as an author and for all the work they have done producing and marketing the book. I reserve special mention for my editor, Elizabeth Brennan, who managed to walk the line between being my saviour and the bane of my life over the past six months. Thanks to Karen Butler, who typed up the first draft of the book and gave us something tangible with which to work from the outset.

I thank Mark McNamara of Morgan Stanley International for his contributions. Fiona Ross of the National Library offered the library as place for uninterrupted writing and thinking, and has also provided facilities at the library for the book launch. I am grateful to Matt Cooper for launching the book.

Dearbhail McDonald, who was also writing her own book, took the time to discuss issues with me and trade information. Thanks to Neil Macdougald for his photography skills.

Accknowledgements

A warm thanks to anyone who has helped me out with this book, and especially to my family and friends for their support and encouragement.

CONTENTS

Contents

INTRODUCTION

Open Dissent

When Lehman Brothers collapsed with liquidity difficulties in the US on Monday, 15 September 2008 it sent shock-waves throughout the financial world. The trust and friendliness of the interbank markets, which were a major source of liquidity for Irish banks, evaporated in front of our eyes. In times of crisis all head offices bring down the shutters to protect home base and this would include recalling major offshore deposits. These offshore deposits made up a great part of Anglo Irish Bank's funding. As they were being withdrawn for whatever reason, the bank was unable to replace them and so needed government assistance. The nervousness and volatility over the next two weeks forced the Government to come out with its guarantee on the deposits and debts of all Irish banks.

This action, while criticised by Europe and the UK, saved the Irish banking system. It was applauded by others around the world including the US Treasury, which felt it was a strong and decisive move, and reduced international concern over the viability of the Irish banks. If the guarantee had not been provided, both domestic and international depositors would have started to pull out, creating a massive liquidity crisis. Keeping pace with the international markets is not an easy task and, as an island economy attached to a European master, putting our self-interest first may not have been politically correct, but it worked.

It might be comforting for many senior people in our community to blame the global markets for the financial crisis in Ireland. After all, we are not big enough to have influence on the global markets and so we may conclude that we are innocent victims. Nothing could be further from reality or the truth. I repeat here a statement that I made at Bank of Ireland's extraordinary general meeting on 27 March 2009: 'While there is a global financial crisis, the crisis that is being experienced in Bank of Ireland has been self-inflicted and not imported.' This applies equally to all six Irish banks.

The Central Bank of Ireland, in its Financial Stability Report produced at the end of 2007 and presented to the Oireachtas in January 2008, identified two key factors that were at the heart of the problem as it was then perceived: liquidity and the credit crunch. These were indeed the key symptoms of a critical disease that was about to beset our nation. But in the presentation to the Oireachtas we were comforted by the forecast of a soft landing. In hindsight it is easy to be critical of this judgment, but I remind those in positions of authority and power that they are paid, often substantial amounts, for foresight as they can only be judged by hindsight. With authority and power comes accountability, whether you are a politician, civil servant, regulator, lawyer, banker, auditor, clergyman or doctor. 'Responsibility' is not difficult to spell or pronounce but it is often unpalatable to take, even in small doses. Those who were empowered to oversee the running of the banks and have seen the destruction of these entities are not the people to be entrusted with the responsibility of turning this critical situation around.

The Central Bank was right in 2007–2008 about the problems of credit and liquidity in the Irish financial system; it simply did not see or did not wish to see the extent of the difficulties. We have experienced the spread of the liquidity crisis across the world in a very short period of time. The crisis is unique in Ireland, however, because of the loose credit standards that existed here, which created a credit bubble. No one forced the banks to create large risky portfolios of commercial and residential mortgages. These mortgages were not being funded by deposits but by overseas short-term funding. This situation – our dependence on overseas funds and poor credit management – meant that when the liquidity crunch hit, Ireland was in a very weak position.

Professor Morgan Kelly, in his paper 'The Irish Credit Bubble',[1] puts forward a very logical and compelling case for the cause of the credit bubble in Ireland. An explosion of bank lending led to predictable rises in the prices of Irish houses and commercial property. In 1995 the average price of a house in Ireland was equal to four years' average industrial earnings. In late 2006, at the peak, new house prices nationally had risen to almost ten years' average earnings while, in Dublin, second-hand prices had risen to seventeen times average yearly earnings. So, what drove the rise in property prices? The cause was excessive bank lending. In his paper Professor Kelly illustrates that mortgages and the availability of credit have a correlation with the increase in house prices. In financial terms, for every additional €1 of mortgage availability, the price of a house increased by €1.13. According to Professor Kelly, rising house prices were driven predominantly by an increase in the size of mortgages that banks were willing to give, with interest rates playing a secondary role and the growth of the population none at all.

For comparative purposes, where the norm for lending in the Eurozone was just over 100 per cent of gross domestic product (GDP), Ireland's bank lending had soared to 200+ per cent of gross national product (GNP) (see Figure 1 in the Appendix). By the end of 2008, the Irish banks were lending vast amounts to property developers and residential mortgagees. The growth in credit relative to GDP created all sorts of distortions in the economy, none greater than the price of houses. The growth in property prices can be viewed from the perspective of increased demand resulting from the increase in population and the low interest levels associated with the euro. Bubbles grow when buyers are motivated by the availability of credit and the hope and expectation that prices will continue to increase. When this spiral of borrowing and increasing prices starts to work in reverse, a problem is created. This would be manageable if it took the form of a slow leak to the bubble, but if there is an edge to this reversal, and this edge is the realisation that prices have peaked, the result is a pricked bubble. As wholesale funding grew to proportions that had not been seen before, the banks became more and more dependent on the rolling over of their wholesale deposits, mostly international short-term deposits, to keep their books in balance.

Common sense would suggest that the combination of easily available mortgages and comparatively low interest rates would create an enormous demand for property. In a developed country the construction sector would normally account for approximately 5 per cent of GDP. The combined contribution of this sector grew to approximately 21 per cent at the peak of the bubble in 2006–2007.[2] Those who had property wanted more, those not yet on the property ladder were assisted by their parents and many, many more just wanted a piece of the action that would hopefully create a nest egg for retirement. The number of second homes in Ireland, i.e. not including holiday homes abroad, amounted to some 300,000 units. This figure presumes that every unit was accounted for in the €60 million raised by the Revenue Commissioners in property tax on second homes in 2009, which, no doubt, wasn't the case.

The side effects of the downturn forced people to re-evaluate where they stood financially with their bankers or fellow investors. Negative equity was an unwelcome visitor into people's homes and investment properties. How did some of these people get to own five, ten, fifteen or even more properties? Take the case of a hard-working public servant who, during the period of prosperity and growth, managed to put a portfolio of properties together that had a market value of €12 million with loans backing these properties of €8 million. This individual was on an annual income in the region of €75,000. One can understand the state of elation when a person manages to acquire a home for each child in the family and in a buoyant market where the value increases every day. However, the downturn came and, instead of being left with a net worth of €4 million, this public servant was potentially bankrupt.[3]

There are similarities between the conditions that existed in property lending, which caused the property bubble in Ireland, and the sovereign debt crisis that we in Europe are faced with today. The principles of lending are the same for every borrower: the lender or investor demands to be repaid in line with the terms of the loan agreement. Many Irish developers are only too aware of this. European sovereign borrowers, who are now either unable or unwilling to repay their loans, face consequences for their economic and political sovereignty. At the moment the money that has been lent by the surplus nations to the deficit nations in Europe is counted by the Bank of International Settlements in US$ trillions. Running deficits have been universally accepted as an economic imperative of consumer-driven expansion or recovery. The concern that now permeates the markets is whether repayment of debts is a realistic part of today's economic equation for growth. The growth of the sovereign debt mountain must be addressed sooner rather than later. Can the debtor nations repay all their current outstanding debt within five, ten, twenty or even fifty years? Should part or all of existing debt be converted into some form of perpetual debt that will ease the burden of repayment? The crisis in Ireland is being magnified as the bank borrowings and sovereign borrowings of the country converge, creating one enormous problem for the state. This is not to suggest that there should be no further borrowings by sovereigns, but would it be too much to ask of governments to adopt the financial discipline they expect of their citizens?

Financial crises have the capacity to magnify the weakest links in the leadership of financial institutions. In my working life, I not only enjoyed a diversified career in financial services, but also a global perspective of the financial markets and the privilege of working directly or indirectly for four remarkable leaders. I not only got to see the strengths and weaknesses of these leaders through daily contact with them, but I also had the experience of seeing them in action and the wisdom of their decision making.

As I look back on my own career in the context of the current crisis, I am struck by the failures that occurred in succession planning in the four major institutions that I have worked for internationally and in Ireland. This issue of succession and leadership is the thread linking Walter Wriston (Citicorp/Citibank, New York), Richard (Dick) Flamson (Security Pacific, California), Donald (Don) Argus (National Australia Bank, Melbourne) and Laurence Crowley (Bank of Ireland, Dublin). Using these four men and these institutions as examples, I wish to describe a common occurrence that may illuminate the machinations of identification and appointment of successors in corporate life, which may in turn provide an insight for those who ask the question, in the context of the current financial crisis, 'What went wrong?'

The first of these leaders was Walter Wriston, chairman and CEO of Citicorp/Citibank (later Citigroup) in the US, which was at one point the largest bank in the world in terms of financial assets. Wriston was very much the doyen of banking and was held in the highest regard by Government, customers, employees, shareholders and, above all, his competitors. He was very much a cerebral visionary. In his fifteen-year term at the helm of Citicorp/Citibank, the organisation grew to be the largest international bank in the world, with a presence in over one hundred countries by the time of his retirement in 1984. His vision of creating a massive international financial services organisation with an equally strong US domestic banking franchise was achieved during his term of office. It was not without its challenges and failures but, in the end, as the reins of the organisation were handed over to John Reed, Citicorp/ Citibank could boast of having an established domestic and international presence in both consumer and wholesale corporate banking.

Globalisation was accelerated under the new leadership. The desire of John Reed to grow a massive diversified financial services company – including an investment banking arm and insurance business through the acquisition of Solomon Brothers and a merger with Travelers

Insurance Company – came about after the 1987 amendment to the Glass–Steagall Act of 1933 (see Chapter 1). The conflicts that occurred due to the difficulty of integrating these various activities resulted in the retirement of John Reed, who was joint head of the institution with Sandy Weill, in 2000. Whatever the differences in style of leadership of the two senior directors, as perceived by the Citicorp board, it was Sandy Weill who survived. The extraordinary growth of this institution over the next seven or eight years resulted in the US Government having to bail out the bank at the onset of the US financial crisis in September 2008. Weill was succeeded by Vikram Pandit in December 2007.

I joined Security Pacific in London in 1985 to set up an international merchant bank. I saw the organisation grow from 2 executives with a small presence in the UK to 3,700 staff in both the debt and equity capital markets, with a presence in 11 financial centres around the world, including New York, London, Frankfurt, Tokyo, Geneva and Sydney. CEO Dick Flamson had a vision at that time which was based on both organic growth and acquisitions. Major brokerage operations in the UK (Hoare Govett), Canada (Burns Fry), New York, Sydney, Tokyo and Frankfurt were identified to complete a global presence. The objective was to create a debt and equity securities capability in each of the major financial centres of the world, thus creating global reach. The challenges were basically twofold: management of cultural differences between major US commercial banks and local foreign brokers in each of the countries, together with the need for substantial capital allocations and strong internal governance for these diverse entities. As in the case of Walter Wriston and Citigroup, when Dick Flamson was ready to hand over the reins of the organisation he did so to an individual in the Security Pacific mould who had come out of the operations and processing side of the bank. His name was Robert (Bob) Smith. His background was domestic US banking with a strong emphasis on operations. The complexities of the capital markets internationally and domestically would lead to the undoing of the global vision. Security Pacific was taken over by Bank of America in 1992 as a result of the poor execution of an acquisition of a major residential property portfolio in Arizona. The suitability of Bob Smith for the role of Flamson's successor was in question from the outset, but the capital and balance sheet challenges that ensued were far too much for the new team to manage. Again, here was a succession plan that appeared set for failure from the beginning.

In 1994 I had the good fortune to join National Australia Bank (NAB) in London with the mandate to develop a profitable wholesale business in the UK and Europe, similar to what I had achieved with Security Pacific but not on the same scale. It was a privilege for me to be appointed to the executive committee of NAB in Melbourne in 1998. Don Argus was the CEO of NAB at the time.

Under Argus's leadership, NAB expanded internationally over time, with the key focus on retail banking. Over several years of expansion, the group had an established presence outside of Australia in England, Ireland, Scotland,

Northern Ireland, the US and New Zealand. Argus's presence was felt throughout the organisation. Here, again, was a fine leader who would prove to be difficult, if not impossible, to replace. By 1999, Argus had decided to move on and was faced with a succession decision. While the proof of Argus's greatness is reflected in his subsequent appointment as chairman of BHP, which became BHP Billiton – the largest mining and resource company in the world – the fate of his beloved NAB was placed in the hands of Frank Cicutto, a NAB employee all his life, who was best described as a credit specialist within the Australian empire. NAB had enjoyed the status of premier bank under Argus for many years but the challenges that beset his successor were enough to see this great institution relegated in the financial league tables. There is an opportunity for a turnaround by the new management team today as the share price currently flounders at levels last experienced some nine years ago.

Another interesting aspect of my time on the executive committee in NAB in Melbourne was the composition of the committee itself. Fred Goodwin, a relatively unknown banker in 1997, was a senior executive on this committee, having spent the previous couple of years as CEO of Clydesdale Bank, a subsidiary of NAB. Fred departed NAB in 1999 when he became deputy chief executive of Royal Bank of Scotland, where he was credited as being the driving force behind the successful takeover of National Westminster Bank in 2002. Fred subsequently became chief executive of Royal Bank of Scotland and was knighted a couple of years later. This bank grew organically and, at Fred's insistence, through acquisition of parts of ABN/ AMRO. This acquisition was opposed by many investors and analysts and was the straw that broke the camel's back. Sir Fred Goodwin, after the crash in late 2008, became the most vilified banker in the UK. Fred believed, in business career terms, that he was in a class of his own. There are few who might argue with that self-assessment today. Anyone who worked with him will know he was an intelligent executive with a strong technical skill base and a single-minded attitude to match. Who in the succession planning process in the Royal Bank of Scotland could have recognised the weaknesses that led to the demise of this great institution under Fred's leadership? Were there any tell-tale signs that were overlooked in the process?

I was fortunate to have Laurence Crowley as Governor (chairman) of Bank of Ireland when I was appointed in 2002 as CEO of the bank. Laurence Crowley had earned a reputation for integrity, good judgment and equally good leadership in Ireland. As an outsider, it was hoped that I could bring change to an organisation that had been founded in 1783 and had developed a strong culture of integrity, respectfulness and industriousness, draped in an Irish flag.

A genuine icon, Bank of Ireland was respected locally and well regarded by regulators and competitors. Innovation was not high on the agenda and a culture of entitlement prevailed. Rank had its privileges. The obligation of earning rather than being entitled was lost in the hundreds of years of institutionalisation within the bank. A fear of change prevailed. What got the bank to where it was in iconic, if not financial, terms was believed to be sufficient. Openly challenging the status quo was not always acceptable as it appeared to reflect disrespect for the past, which had made the institution what it was. I introduced cost management programmes early in my tenure, which fundamentally put the freedom of choice in terms of cars, travel and incidental expenses back into the hands of the employees. This was not met with enthusiasm as the culture of entitlement was ever comforting.

Again, in the arena of succession planning, with my sudden departure from Bank of Ireland in 2004 after some two years and eight months at the helm, I am left wondering to this day as to what is the level of preparedness needed from a board's perspective to ensure an uncomplicated transition at chief executive level. In the interest of protecting this great institution that I had come to admire, I was faced with an incredible dilemma when information pertaining to access to an adult website by myself was released to the *Sunday Business Post* on the last weekend in May 2004. I made the only decision I could in order to protect the reputation of the institution. The release of this information occurred some 8 weeks after 500 technology jobs in the bank were outsourced to Hewlett Packard. To this day I do not know where the leak sprung from. In my judgment, no personal reputation was worth the effects the potential salacious coverage of this story might have had on the corporate reputation of Ireland's financial icon. That being the case, considering the time pressures, the Court (board) had few options. The obvious internal candidate for succession was Brian Goggin; an external search was unlikely to identify a better candidate. He was the most experienced internal candidate and was viewed as a safe pair of hands in this time of turmoil, since I had departed the bank instantly. In the interests of corporate performance, no CEO deserves to pay the price, in terms of health, that Brian Goggin has.

Who could have expected that the board, which had accepted my resignation on the grounds of protecting the reputation of the bank, would have overseen, under a new chairman and CEO, the irreparable damage done to Bank of Ireland's reputation and, more so, to the reputation of the country over recent years? The fingerprints of all those who are responsible for the failure of the bank to withstand the current crisis are easily identified. Many are still on the board. I consider open dissent to be my responsibility and obligation.

The identification and appointment of key executives and in particular CEOs has to be seen as the most important responsibility of the chairperson and the nominations committee in any public financial institution. What these examples above show is that mistakes can be made at board level in the appointment of leaders. The pattern of a respected and able leader being replaced by someone who doesn't have the capacity to take a corporation through whatever challenges arise may have to do with the successor being appointed at a time when the corporation is confident and in a strong position. In this situation, having someone at the helm with different qualities to the previous leader is perhaps not seen as a problem. The process of succession needs to be examined in major financial institutions to see where improvements can be made to safeguard the long-term viability of the institutions.

After a lifetime of banking in the Irish and international markets, I can reflect on my experiences and offer observations and suggestions for the survival of financial institutions in Ireland in the long term. As I recount my experiences with leaders in the financial community and observe the failures of institutions, I must conclude that some institutions can become too large to manage. Perhaps it would be clearer to say that, beyond a certain size, the complexities of managing major financial institutions accentuate the multiple risks undertaken. Few executives have the experience or skill base to manage complex financial institutions, so one may conclude that constraining banks from becoming systemic risks is the best safeguard to protect the financial system in a country in the long term.

During my time at Citicorp/Citibank, Security Pacific, National Australia Bank and Bank of Ireland, a lot of time, effort and money were invested in the pursuit of the creation of a code of behaviour and the establishment of corporate values. These pursuits are often deemed to be futile by those who believe the introspective nature of these activities to be boring and tedious. But if board members and the executive management of an organisation cannot stand by its enshrined values and standards, it is unlikely that the rest of the employees will. Within a bank, there must be a clear vision for the direction of the organisation, which is communicated clearly to all stakeholders; integrity in all dealings; a strong capital base; an acceptance of change; a culture of sensible corporate governance; an unending hunger to be best in class; and, to make all this possible, a strong leader who is respected by all.

When the dust clears on the nationalisations and bankruptcies in the banking world, an examination of those leaders who failed or came through the crisis somewhat scathed would make interesting reading. Good leadership, not just in banking but at the highest political level, is the key to our recovery.

Here are the characteristics we don't want in our leaders, but which have unfortunately been demonstrated by some of them over recent years:

- Say one thing and mean another.
- Act in accordance with hidden agendas.
- Prefer to look good rather than doing the right thing.
- Personal needs are put ahead of the good of society.

However, there are behaviours that have been accepted over time as good leadership practice across all professions and sectors of society. The one characteristic that can be identified in all good leaders is authenticity, which is reflected in the following:

- Communicate honestly and wisely.
- Their actions match their words.
- Say clearly what they believe and stand for.

- Respect and uphold people's dignity.
- Treat people fairly and equitably.

Having standards that we agree on, such as the checklist above, makes our judgment of our leaders more balanced and consistent. Some may think that it is too idealistic to have such a code of behaviour, but surely we should have something to aspire to.

Whether in the political, corporate or even domestic arenas, leaders are constantly under pressure for results from their followers. To maintain a position of power, leaders may often make decisions that favour the short-term solution with scant regard for the value of long-term planning. Governments and companies need to maintain balance between the long- and short-term goals of their constituents in order to survive. Sustainable prosperity requires a long-term view, which frequently means that certain short-term decisions have to be subordinated in favour of long-term goals. Success is unlikely to be achieved by frequent abrupt changes in strategy, which are symptomatic of a lack of long-term vision. Simply put, leaders should articulate clear plans to the shareholders or the electorate and any short-term decisions taken should be viewed within a long-term time frame. A clear communication plan needs to be in place so that people understand that what is politically favourable cannot be put ahead of what is in the best long-term interests of society. As a leader, you shouldn't underestimate your stakeholders; they will stay with you for the long term if you explain your decisions in the context of a long-term time horizon.

This applies equally to corporate leaders and politicians and it might be best summarised in the following quote: 'Good leaders achieve results; great leaders achieve sustainable results by serving multiple constituencies.'[4]

Viewing with hindsight the political and banking environments that incubated the current financial crisis, one can see that a lack of moral fibre was allowed to flourish through a culture of silent dissent. This culture, which favours silence over openness, pervades the boards of our corporations, our Government and our political parties. Bad decisions are made because good people say nothing. It is a culture deeply associated with cronyism. Silent dissent is, I believe, central to the reasons for the severity of the banking crisis in Ireland and why we got caught at a disadvantage in 2008. In this book, as a protest against this culture, I wish to exercise the opposite – open dissent.

Open Dissent counters the culture of denial at all levels of our community, from the banking sector to the political and public sectors. Identifying the extent of our economic and financial problems is the first step to remedying them, and remedies are what this book is essentially about.

Chapter 1 goes back as far as the Great Depression to analyse the origins of the banking crisis in the US. How and why the crisis has manifested itself as it has in Ireland is the subject of Chapter 2, while Chapter 3 looks closely at the culture of silent dissent in this country, which leads to a discussion on corporate governance, how it has failed in Ireland and what the standards should be. The controversial question of who should pay for the crisis is broached against the background of a discussion on fairness in society in Chapter 4. However, pointing the finger is not constructive in the long term; an understanding of what went wrong and how we can move forward is, of course, more important. Chapter 5 is concerned with the conditions that will bring about recovery, including a look at changing the bankruptcy laws and encouraging informed investment. The controversial subject of the National Asset Management Agency (NAMA) is discussed in Chapter 6, which, if the Swedish model in the 1990s is anything to go by (Chapter 7), should be an effective machine to get Ireland out of the crisis, as long as transparency is respected and common sense prevails. Chapter 8 introduces the idea for a brand new banking model, while Chapter 9 looks at Ireland's recovery and the issue of sovereign debt in the context of the European Union (EU).

I am often asked, 'Did you see the crisis coming?' I can respond that I have written about it and spoken to many people over the past three years on the subject, whether in the newspapers, on the radio or on TV. My comments reflected a real concern for the impending financial and economic crisis and, once we became aware of the damage done, the steps that should be taken for recovery. A second question that is often posed along with the first is, 'If you were still in banking in recent years, would you have done anything differently?' To this I can only say that I was not there at the time decisions were being made and I therefore can take neither blame nor credit.

However, I will say that Bank of Ireland was established in 1783 and, through modest growth over 221 years, the balance sheet reached €100 billion in assets by 2004; four years later, in 2008, the bank's balance sheet had doubled to more than €200 billion. The accelerated growth can only be attributed to the ambitious desires of the executive management and board.

I often compare my mindset as a CEO of a bank to my mindset as an independent investor today. In both positions I can only be judged by the financial scorecard that reflects my gains and losses. I have no hesitation disclosing that I lost millions during this chaotic period on investments in Bank of Ireland, Royal Bank of Scotland and Allied Irish Banks (AIB). Having crystallised my losses, I have actively managed my financial position through trading in shares and foreign exchange to recover a large percentage of my capital and dividends. I would hope this activity reflects a mindset of market awareness and a penchant for action. My fingers are on the pulse of the market and all I can hope is that this keeps me better informed for investment decisions. I firmly believe that, had I still been in banking, I would not have remained in denial for long, or, if appearances are anything to go by, at least not as long as Ireland's executive directors.

CHAPTER 1

Birth of a Crisis

It may appear strange at first glance that we need to go back to the Great Depression of 1929–1933 to find a major contributory factor to the financial crisis in Ireland today. How banking changed and evolved over the past eighty or so years owes a lot to the Banking Act of 1933, more commonly known as the Glass–Steagall Act, which was passed in the US as a reaction to the collapse of a large portion of the US commercial banking system. The repeal of this Act in 1999 helped create the banking environment that allowed for the international financial crisis that began in 2008.

While recessions are experienced throughout the world from time to time, a depression is a rarity. Defining the difference between these two economic terms is not easy for one simple reason – a universally accepted definition does not exist. A recession is when your neighbour loses his job, but a depression is when you lose yours, or so the line goes.

The standard definition of a recession is a decline in the GDP of a country for two or more consecutive quarters. It is an unsatisfactory explanation as it does not take into consideration changes in other variables such as unemployment rates or consumer confidence. An economic recovery that doesn't lead to more employment is merely a mirage. Also, using quarterly data makes it difficult to pinpoint when the recession begins and ends.

There are those who would define a recession as a fall in business activity until it bottoms out, following a period when it had reached its peak. When business activity begins to rise again and an expansionary period is experienced, the recession has come to an end. By this definition, the average recession lasts about one year. Many economists would agree with this.

The term 'recession' was developed to differentiate periods like the Great Depression from smaller economic declines, implying a relatively simple definition of a depression as a recession that lasts longer and sees a larger decline in business activity. So, in the context of changes in GDP, a depression occurs when real GDP declines by more than 10 per cent.

The Great Depression came about in the context of massive speculative trading coming off the back of a five-year bull market. The bull market came to an end in September 1929 and trading climaxed on Black Thursday, 24 October 1929, with almost 13,000,000 shares being traded. Panic selling followed on Monday and Tuesday, 28 and 29 October 1929, which concluded in total losses of US$30 billion – ten times the federal budget and more than the US spent on World War I. Personal and corporate savings fell from US$15.3 billion to US$2.3 billion.[5]

Protectionism was unlikely to have been a main cause of the Depression but it surely helped the spread of its effects throughout the developed world. Increased tariffs, intended to protect local manufacturing and farming communities, fostered global protectionism and resulted in world trade declining by 60 per cent between 1929 and 1934.[6]

It is often overlooked that the last depression by our definition in the US was during 1937–38, when GDP declined by 18.2 per cent.[7] The effects of these economic circumstances made the US economy dependent on the war machine and military expansion to fill the domestic coffers. The sector that would create the greatest economic stimulus was armaments. Commentators have broached the subject that the US decision to enter World War II was based somewhat on economic motives. But perhaps this is a cynical take on what lay behind the political decisions at that time.

In the 1930s people were not exposed to technology in the way we are today. For example, the time it took to report one quarter's GDP figures or the previous year's figures would have been measured in months if not years. However, the evidence was clear that there was a depression being experienced by the length of the dole queues and the number of soup kitchens. The hardships and misery experienced in the 1930s laid the foundations for a more sympathetic response to the plight of the less fortunate in the US thereafter. People whose wealth had evaporated and whose life savings were depleted or were lost in a banking system that was not prepared or robust enough to withstand the fallout of the economic disaster were faced with a bleak future.

In the period leading up to the Depression, a five-year bull market had created a highly competitive market in both debt and equity. The equity markets were primarily the preserve of the investment banks, while debt was the principal focus of the commercial banks. During this time, a combination of greed and pressure from investors for increased returns prompted the commercial banks to ease into the investment banks' preserve of equity. In times of economic growth the commercial banks found themselves providing major US corporations with equity, loans, board memberships and a variety of advisory activities. The equity of the commercial banks was now inextricably linked to the future prospects of these corporations. When the economy turned for the worse, the banks were faced with enormous conflicts of interest as they held various roles with their corporate customers, from equity stake-holders to lenders. As the need for more capital grew in the early days of the Depression, decisions were made to increase the commercial banks' shareholdings in corporations suffering from the downturn; deposits were now being used in the higher risk area of corporate equity rather than in the traditional loan markets.

This injection of the banks' capital and deposits into corporate America was the rock on which commercial banking perished in the Great Depression. The banks had to follow bad investments in companies with increased loan facilities in the hope that the companies with deteriorating balance sheets and profit and loss accounts would recover. When circumstances got worse, they were faced with the same decision again – to increase the loans or see their equity written off in bankruptcies. In many instances, the equity, loans and many other forms of support were written off, which led to the collapse of such corporations and, in turn, the banks themselves.

A retail bank acts as a principal in the context of dealing with customers. When people deposit money in a bank they are actually lending the money to the bank. In the event the bank lends this money on to a borrower who fails to repay, the bank's capital is used to absorb these losses and hence the depositor does not lose out. Unfortunately, if the bank's capital is not adequate enough to absorb cumulative loans and investment losses, the depositor's funds are put at risk.

The other side of this equation is the role of investment banks. These banks don't use depositors' money as they are not licensed to raise deposits from the retail market. They attract funds from investors who, through due diligence, are able to evaluate the underlying risks of investments undertaken by the investment banks. The investment banks receive substantial fees for their efforts. In this situation, the investor lends (debt) or invests (equity) in the opportunity presented by the investment bank directly with the issuer. In the event of the issuer failing to repay, the original investor will lose some or all of his investment. The relationship of the investment bank to the investor is one of an agent and not a principal. Thus, there is no recourse by the investor unless malfeasance can be proved.

This area of corporate debt and equity has been a financial battleground for commercial and investment banks over the years. The Glass–Steagall Act of 1933 separated the activities of commercial and investment banks. It also provided for the foundation of the Federal Deposit Insurance Corporation for the protection of bank deposits.

Over the next sixty-six years efforts were made to repeal the Glass–Steagall Act. Cases were made for and against its repeal. In 1987, the major US banks actively lobbied Washington to repeal the Act as they wanted to expand their corporate strategies by offering what were viewed as essential products to their major customers. This business activity was viewed as an enormous potential revenue generator for the banks. The arguments raised for the preservation of the Act ranged from conflicts of interest leading to the abuses to which the Act was a response in the first place, to protection of depositors and questions as to whether commercial banks were equipped to handle the risk profile of securities, which was different to that of loans. An amendment to the Act enabled the commercial banks to enter the underwriting of corporate equities in a limited way at this time.

On the other hand, well-structured arguments against the preservation of the Act were put forward, with regard to depository institutions that were operating in a deregulated financial market in which the lines between loans, securities and deposits were not well drawn. The commercial banks were losing market share to securities firms which were gradually expanding their presence in the raising of debt and equity for sovereigns, corporations and financial institutions. The argument of the banks for the repeal of the Act was not about good customer service; it was about tens of billions of dollars in revenue. However, if the Act was repealed, would the banks, as new entrants in this particular market, be winners or were the risks so complex that they might have to pay a very heavy entry price?

On 12 November 1999 the repeal of Glass–Steagall was signed into law by President Bill Clinton after years of lobbying by the various interested parties. As part of the background noise to all the debates was the promise that the securities industry could be used to provide mortgages to millions of poor Americans who might otherwise not be able to own their own homes. This was high on the agenda of all Democrats but none could imagine what the toxic mix of subprime debt, structured investment vehicles (SIVs), credit default swaps (CDSs), collateralized debt obligations (CDOs) and derivatives would lead to.

The repeal of the Act enabled commercial lenders such as Citigroup, the largest US bank in 1999, to underwrite and trade the fastest growing instruments in the history of the financial markets. The author Elizabeth Warren, one of the five outside experts who constitute the Congressional Oversight Panel of the Troubled Asset Relief Program (TARP), has commented that the repeal of this Act contributed to the global financial crisis of 2008–2009. The year before the repeal, subprime loans were just 5 per cent of all mortgage lending. By the time the credit crisis peaked in 2008, they were approaching 30 per cent.[8]

An interesting aspect was that, a short time after the repeal of the Glass–Steagall Act, new, complex products were created which enabled millions of families in America to purchase and own their own homes. What had changed? Commercial banks, which once would not have considered this subprime market as a suitable credit risk, were now pouring billions into it. The investment banks created vehicles that were wrapped in credit default swaps, had very modest amounts of equity and were rated AAA by the large rating agencies. The funding of these vehicles was often through the excess deposits that were in the vaults of the commercial banks – a tragedy in the making. The rating agencies fundamentally replaced the traditional credit process in the banks. No longer did questions of a borrower's ability and willingness to repay need to be addressed, as the answers were implied by the AAA rating assigned to the mortgages by the rating agencies.

The origins of complex products can be traced back some thirty years when some colleagues of mine at Citicorp Investment Bank Ltd in London carried out the first ever derivative transaction. Shortly thereafter, I was also involved in carrying out these transactions and eighteen months later I became global head of derivatives in New York. There was a team of us in London and New York who forged bonds in both professional and friendship terms. This transaction in 1980 was the birth of a new industry in financial instruments. In the early days of derivatives no one could have ever imagined the potential of these new products. The term 'financial engineering' was introduced at the time to describe the creation of these transactions because of the very complex nature of most of them. Originally there were two types of derivatives or swaps: interest rate and currency.

In their simplest form, swaps were to facilitate the customer who wished to raise fixed-rate borrowings but could only do so at prohibitive rates, and thus was left with the alternative of having to pay a variable rate. The uncertainty of variable rates often forced capital projects to be reconsidered or deferred due to the customer's inability to budget accurately for the total cost of the finance over the period of the loan. Necessity is the mother of invention. Banks were able to identify customers wishing to borrow floating or variable rate funds but who had the capacity to raise fixed-rate funds inexpensively. Some of these customers had enormous capacity to raise fixed interest funds at preferential rates in the capital markets. These capital market issuers were normally governments, major corporations or financial institutions. At a prearranged price, two borrowers could swap their interest payments, fixed for floating, and so the birth of the derivatives (swaps) market occurred. The financial engineering skills involved in the pricing and structuring of these transactions through the bond markets were finely honed, so that each party got what they wanted at a cheaper price due to the perceived credit rating of each party to the transaction in the marketplace.

As customers became more educated in the area, the deals grew in size and frequency. Deals in the early days would be executed for amounts of US$25 million to

US$50 million. In 1982, I wrote a paper for Citibank Research which forecasted that this new market had the potential of growing by €1 billion per year. During my time in New York as head of global derivatives this activity expanded beyond all expectations. The expert of the group and managing director of Citicorp Investment Bank in the UK was David Pritchard, an individual whose name became synonymous with the business and the international capital markets. His background as an aeronautical engineer served him well through a most illustrious career in financial services before he retired as vice-chairman of Lloyds TSB. He was brought onto the board of AIB in 2007 and is chairman of AIB (UK) Ltd today. There is unlikely to be a better financial brain or experienced bank director in the country and I hope his talents will be used extensively in the restructuring of the banking system in Ireland.

The derivatives market broadened from being based on interest rates and foreign currency in the early years to encompass equity and credit default swaps. Little did the minds behind the first derivatives realise that they would become a multi-trillion dollar business. The origins of the derivatives business was in a corporate finance environment where financial solutions were sought for customers who wished to reduce the cost of borrowings or increase their yields on investments. Sophisticated mathematical programmes were developed and the efforts in the early days to get two customers with equal but opposite positions disappeared with the creation of a marketplace better known as the warehouse in each bank. In effect, government bonds were being used as a counterparty in a transaction. The expansion of the market was attributable to the fact that, through a variety of hedging techniques and financial programmes, a level of liquidity was created that no one could have visualised early on. Many point their finger at this financial area as having the potential to cause the next global financial crisis. This could be the case, but the precautions that are being taken and considered by the regulators and market participants should reduce the likelihood of a catastrophe. There is no telling, however, how foolish people can act through the motive of greed. These markets in derivatives are now truly global with a large menu of products that provide governments, corporations and financial institutions with the tools to manage their balance sheets more effectively by limiting their risk exposure. The risk management element of derivatives has given way to the weight of trading in the provision of liquidity in these instruments. A single derivative may be traded a thousand times in its life.

The traditional distribution network for mortgages in the US was through the branches of national, regional and local banks. Mortgage brokers had a modest input into this market compared to what they ended up with when the floodgates for mortgages were opened through the creation of structured investment vehicles. With these new vehicles, access to credit was ever present. Families were approached with all forms of, often complex, mortgage offerings. Homeownership, everyone's dream, was now possible for thousands. The corruption in the selling of mortgages

became everyday practice. Families were approached with
an offering for a mortgage to buy a new home and at the end
of the discussions they were on their way to owning a fully
furnished house with a new car in the driveway. These were
the 100 per cent plus (subprime) mortgages with initial
monthly repayments less than the mortgagee had previously been paying for rental accommodation. How could
this be? The mortgagers offered low interest rates for the
first two or three years, which would be re-priced upwards
to two or three times (or some other multiple) the original
rate in due course. But when you are sitting in your new
home with a new car in your driveway, it is difficult to pon-
der anything other than your good fortune.

The day of reckoning always arrives. People who had
lived a dream for a couple of years could only watch as the
bailiffs arrived to repossess their homes because they
could not afford to meet their increased monthly mortgage
repayments.

As demanded by the politicians in Washington, the pace
of loan modifications was accelerated, which spared hundreds of thousands of families from the hardship of losing
their homes. Financial competitors were cooperating with
one another to get troubled homeowners to contact their
mortgage providers or servicers and, in turn, to find a way
to accommodate the requirements of both parties where possible. In an Irish context this might be considered as NAMA
2. To put this into context, these moves to protect the mortgagees occurred in 2008–2009 when Ireland was already in
a depression but still waiting for action to be taken.

The US's battle to save its banking system, which was on the verge of collapse, was achieved by political negotiation, intelligent corporate solutions and strong, capable people who were competent decision makers. Had the US not come out of this potential meltdown, the global systemic effect would have been catastrophic. Two books, *Too Big to Fail: Inside the Battle to Save Wall St* by Andrew Ross Sorkin[9] and *On the Brink: Inside the Race to Stop the Collapse of the Global Financial System* by Hank Paulson,[10] provide valuable insight into this turbulent period. When the crisis struck in 2008, Hank Paulson was the US Treasury Secretary, unquestionably the most powerful financial position in the world. On the occasion of President Obama's inauguration in Washington in January 2009, Paulson was replaced by Timothy Geitner.

Paulson has had time to reflect on what lessons were learned that could help the US avoid a recurrence of such a disaster in the future. His reflections on his experiences in 2007–2008 led him to lay out the following principles,[11] which are equally applicable to the Irish market:

The structural economic imbalances among the major economies of the world that led to massive cross-border capital flows are an important source of the justly criticised excesses in their financial system. These imbalances lay at the root of the crisis. Simply put, in the United States we save much less than we consume. This forces us to borrow large amounts of money from oil-exporting countries or from Asian nations, like China and Japan, with high saving rates and low shares of domestic consumption. The crisis has abated, but these imbalances persist and must be addressed.

Our regulatory system remains a hopelessly outmoded patchwork quilt built for another day and age. It is rife with duplication, gaping holes and counterproductive competition among regulators. The system hasn't kept pace with financial innovation and needs to be fixed so that we have the capacity and the authority to respond to constantly evolving global capital markets.

The financial system contained far too much leverage, as evidenced by inadequate cushions of both capital and liquidity. Much of the leverage was imbedded in largely opaque, complex financial products. Today it is generally understood that banks and investment banks in the US, Europe, and the rest of the world did not have enough capital. Less well understood is the important role that liquidity needs to play in bolstering the safety and stability of banks. The credit crisis exposed widespread reliance on poorer liquidity practices, notably a dependence on unstable short-term funding. Financial institutions that rely heavily on short-term borrowings need to have plenty of cash on hand for bad times. And many didn't. Inadequate liquidity cushions, I believe, were a bigger problem than inadequate capital levels.

The largest financial institutions are so big and complex that they pose a dangerously large risk. Today the top 10 financial institutions in the US hold close to 60 per cent of the national financial assets, up from 10 per cent in 1990. This dramatic concentration, coupled with much greater interconnectedness, means that the failure of any of a few very large institutions can take down a big part of the system and, in domino fashion, topple the rest. The concept of 'too big to fail'[12] has moved from the academic literature to reality and must be addressed.

When President Obama took office in January 2009, he was able to look back at a financial landscape strewn with eight major institutions,[13] now no longer in existence, that had once formed the bedrock of US financial services, and the five major investment banks that had either been taken over, had gone bankrupt or had become bank holding companies. The measures taken by the previous administration were decisive, which may have been the salvation of the global financial markets. President Obama sought the assistance of Paul Volcker, who introduced what is described as the Volcker Rule, a proposal to limit the size of financial firms and to stop the risky activities of banks.

On 25 June 2010, the Dodd–Frank Bill, which implements most of the proposals put forward by Volcker, was agreed by Congress and was subsequently passed in July 2010. Most people in the marketplace refer to the Dodd–Frank Wall Street Reform and Consumer Protection Act as a reintroduction of the Glass–Steagall Act or a facsimile thereof, because ultimately it separates and limits the activities of banks. The Act makes broad changes to the existing regulatory structure, streamlining it and creating new regulatory agencies. The object of the Act is to address and eliminate the loopholes that led to the economic crisis and to protect the economy, investors, businesses and the taxpayer. The Act ends the bailout of financial institutions by the taxpayer.

Among other restrictions, the Act prevents banks that have a direct or indirect relationship with a hedge fund or private equity fund from entering a transaction with the fund without disclosing the full extent of the relationship to the regulating entity. It also puts limits on the activities and transactions that may be conducted by nonbank financial companies. The Act explicitly limits the largest financial companies in terms of growth by acquisition. No financial company will be permitted to merge with another company if the total consolidated liabilities of the combined company would exceed 10 per cent of the total liabilities of the financial system. This changes the emphasis from deposits to total liabilities, which acknowledges other sources of funding used by the market.

The Act's restrictions on some types of proprietary trading by banking firms may lead banks to reconsider their status. Under the bailout of the US financial system on 22 September 2008, investment banks Goldman Sachs and Morgan Stanley became bank holding companies. The benefits associated with proprietary trading has greater relevance to Goldman Sachs than Morgan Stanley with regard to their respective operating performances. Today, Morgan Stanley has moved away from proprietary trading as a main activity in its business model. The Act may be the catalyst for Goldman Sachs to consider going back to its roots as a private partnership.

The aftershock of the liquidity crisis of 2008–2009 continues to be felt today. It is comforting for some to believe that the liquidity crisis that had its roots in the US financial system and that spread across the world with speed was at the heart of the Irish banking meltdown. There is no doubt that when confidence is lost in banking, liquidity dries up immediately. Ask any businessperson today how difficult it is to get liquidity for his or her small or medium enterprise

(SME). However, as mentioned, we cannot blame the global crisis for what happened and is still happening in Ireland. The effects of the liquidity crisis in Ireland may well be a continued downward spiral in property prices and a prolonged period of deflation. Our international reputation, earned and built over a sixteen-year period and that saw us reach the highest levels of credit ratings in the world, has been swiftly reversed.

Very powerful people all over the world sang the praises of the Celtic Tiger. We had achieved the status of 'most enviable nation' for the speed at which we moved from stagnancy to prosperity. The economic miracle that was created and that flourished for sixteen years earned respect and admiration throughout the financial world. Many cynics would have us believe that we were blessed with massive investments from Europe, without which we would not have succeeded. True or false, we invested and managed these funds to the betterment of our society. The reputation that we earned was that of an educated, hard-working, energetic, innovative workforce. Circumstances have tarnished this image but it is in our own hands to use these qualities to drive our recovery. Through various government bodies, the Industrial Development Agency (IDA), Enterprise Ireland and others, we managed to catch wave after wave in the changing economic world through intelligent planning and execution of such plans. We can do it again, but we need the leaders in all areas of our society working together to achieve a common goal – recovery.

Paying the piper in the financial markets has been almost instant, but our decision-making abilities often lag behind. As the Government continues to drip feed bad news about future tax cuts sprinkled with hopeful messages about a jobless recovery, one must really wonder what our leaders are about, and if we have any alternatives. The Americans were able to make their decisions quickly, which saved their country and, in turn, the global financial markets. Whether these actions will lead to a deferred double dip in the economy, only time will tell. Forecasting is better left to meteorologists.

It was old-fashioned teamwork that enabled the recession-damaged Swedish economy to recover in the 1990s as all parties put the good of the country ahead of political parties or personal agendas (see Chapter 7). The concept of working together is not ingrained in the culture of politics and public service in this country. The key parties to our crisis are bankers, developers, regulators, politicians and civil servants. If they believe they can create a long-term solution to our country's economic problems without talking to one another, they are sadly mistaken. Too often the political agenda is put forward as a reason for the various parties not consulting one another. The somewhat dictatorial attitude of the Department of Finance and its colleagues in NAMA needs to be questioned and reined in. They do not have the experience or wit to create solutions that will re-instill confidence and trust in Ireland's commercial market. The need for a collaborative approach between key parties – bankers, developers and NAMA – is essential to see us out of this crisis.

CHAPTER 2

A View from Dame Street – The Crisis in Ireland

On 10 December 2007 I visited the Governor of the Central Bank of Ireland in the presence of the two executive directors who were responsible for the issuance of the Financial Stability Report that had been published a few weeks earlier. I had come to discuss this report. All EU nations provide a status report annually for the European Central Bank (ECB), which in turn is consolidated into an EU report. As each country focuses on the strengths and challenges in their domestic financial market, any weaknesses can be subsequently addressed with or without input from Europe. In their Financial Stability Report of November 2007, the Central Bank of Ireland recognised liquidity and the credit crunch as market concerns that required observation. The outcome of the meeting on 10 December was simple and reassuring – we were in for a 'soft landing'. I dissented and I expressed myself accordingly.

On 30 January 2008 the Central Bank of Ireland presented its Financial Stability Report to the Oireachtas.

During this presentation the twin challenges of liquidity and the credit crunch were addressed. However, in conclusion, the report and the Governor made the judgment that the country was in for a soft landing and that we did not have to worry. On 29 September 2008, some eight months later, all the debts of the Irish banking system were guaranteed by the Government to prevent the genuine threat of a meltdown of the Irish banking system.

One week earlier, and following on from the meeting of December 2007, I wrote the following letter to Governor Hurley. The letter indicates the level of my anxiety and concern in 2007–2008 over the deterioration of the financial markets. In fairness to the Governor, the pressurised environment at that time left him little opportunity to respond to my concerns.

22 September 2008

Central Bank and Financial Services
   Authority of Ireland
Dame Street
Dublin 2

Re: Market Stability

Dear Governor,

Since we met in December 2007 I have given considerable and continual thought to the stability of the financial markets and the many causes behind our present situation. My worst fears were realised this morning with the news of the two remaining US investment banks (Goldman Sachs and Morgan Stanley) being authorised to become bank holding companies. This, I believe, is truly the worst thing to happen to the financial markets.

Investment banks traditionally deal with investors and have done so since the early 1900s under the adage *caveat emptor*. This implies very clearly that the informed investor is aware of the risks their money is being used for. The [retail] banks, on the other hand, have for a long time dealt with depositors' money with due consideration of their fiduciary responsibilities to this constituency. I don't have to tell you or anyone within the bank that the primary reason for the regulatory framework in relation to banking is to ensure that depositors' money is protected and the payment system safeguarded.

Investment banks, in my belief, have not had a culture of concern for their investors (as reflected in the recent turmoil) other than an attitude that could be reflected in the following – 'When we bring you a deal there are risks attached and both of us share in these on an equity basis.'

Letting the investment banks into the preserve of bank holding companies with the right to attract depositors' money is akin to letting the fox into the hen house to arrange its next meal! This recent proposal from Mr Hank Paulson to ensure the liquidity of the investment banks is perceived not to be impaired, in fact puts the fate of the depositors at risk. Somehow, to achieve stability in the market, there is a perception being created that, with having the ex-investment banks now regulated as bank holding companies, our worst fears of a meltdown will be avoided. I believe these actions simply give us a deferment of a problem rather than a solution.

If regulation is required to control the activities of the banking community then the unpalatable but possibly more attractive solution would be the reintroduction of the Glass–Steagall Act. The dilution of this Act during the 1980s and 1990s, which led to the repeal of the Act in 1999, in my judgment, has been at the heart of the current turmoil in the marketplace.

As you may recall in our conversation last December, I mentioned that the liquidity crisis and the credit crunch were symptoms and not the principal illness that we were experiencing. I have contended for some time that the real problem has been the intrusion of the investment banks into the traditional banking marketplace. They achieve this through the creation of sophisticated, highly engineered products, which were very highly leveraged while being made to look attractive to mortgagees on the one hand, and to investors and depositors on the other. The lack of confidence that has grown out of these products has led to the consequent liquidity and credit problems. The current situation appears to have a lot in common with 1929–33. Unfortunately I think we are only, in relative terms, in 1931 … a couple of years to go!

For the sake of brevity I attach my own conclusions on a single sheet to this letter as to the principal causes of the current state of instability in the marketplace. I would be more than pleased to discuss at length or briefly my suggestions as to the solutions that should be adopted to prevent a recurrence of this situation with your colleagues or anyone else who you may feel appropriate.

Yours sincerely,

_____

Michael D. Soden

The contents of the attached sheet were:

'Potential Meltdown in the Marketplace'

Who caused the current situation?
The investment banks, hedge funds, rating agencies and brokers in various linked ways managed to create the current situation. There are more participants to this dilemma but the principal protagonists are those mentioned.

Why did it happen?
A combination of astute financial engineering and creative accounting, together with a culture of excessive greed, were the principal ingredients.

What caused this to happen?
Excessive leverage and unfettered abuse of this age-old corporate finance technique are at fault. It could also be put down to the delayed consequences of the repeal of the Glass–Steagall Act.

How did this occur?
Through lack of regulation and control of investment banks whose creativity, energy and ingenuity went awry. It must be highlighted that the investment banks were aided in their frenzied development of the securities market by the extremely poor judgment of the rating agencies. The excessive use of the technique of shorting the market has contributed substantially to the acceleration of the current market instability.

Solution:
A reintroduction of the Glass–Steagall Act or facsimile thereof, which controls and monitors the liquidity and capital structures of the investment banks, would be the first step in a two-part strategy. The second step would be a constraint placed on the banking sector with regard to providing any monies through the interbank market to the investment banks, together with a restriction on the banks investing in any leveraged securities.

I stand by my recommendations in the above document.

The crisis that started in the US financial system in August 2007 was going to have far greater impact on the rest of the world than most would have imagined and forecasted. It would appear that, while we listen to forecasts and commentaries on all areas of the international markets, the tendency is to only hear that which suits our own domestic outlook. We had decided that we were in for a soft landing, because anything else would be politically unpalatable and unpatriotic.

It is true that the Central Bank would have given warnings to the Irish banks as regards the overheating of the commercial and residential property sectors. It seems that the six Irish banks – Bank of Ireland, Anglo Irish Bank, AIB, Irish Life and Permanent, EBS Building Society and Irish Nationwide – did not fully listen to the advice of the Central Bank. It is likely that they only heard what they wanted to hear, that we were in for a soft landing. The lack of action taken by the banks was not out of disrespect for the Central Bank but more likely because of the demands for increased profits from their shareholders.

While macro-economic factors were at play globally in 2007 and the first half of 2008, Ireland was feeling comfortable and the six banking institutions were still aggressive in their lending. No one believed that there was a liquidity problem in the Irish banks and, furthermore, there was an unquenchable thirst for credit. Developers who had been successful in Ireland over the previous ten to fifteen years found the market at home less attractive than places far away. Many wealthy Irish developers engaged in international diversification, setting themselves up as property experts in places as far-flung and diverse as Dubai, Abu Dhabi, Hong Kong, Chicago and many other locations, the names of which were unfamiliar and difficult to pronounce. Developers became like Christopher Columbus looking for a New World for their ever-increasing wealth. Was this a signal for them to recognise that the Irish market had peaked and, with the assistance of bankers, they could venture abroad? Developers may not have been aware of what they were embarking on, but they were fast becoming diversified risk managers.

On 28 September 2008 the Government of Ireland was faced with this very critical problem: major corporate wholesale deposits were being withdrawn from Anglo Irish Bank and it was clear that they could not be replaced as quickly as they were being withdrawn. The contagion effect of this was the likelihood of other banks failing and, in turn, the country being put at risk. The decision and speed of putting in place a guarantee for the debts was appropriate at that time and preserved the country from a fate worse than the alternative, which was a potential collapse of the market. Only those who were involved will ever fully understand the various forces at work and the perceived risk to the country when the decision to issue the guarantee was made.

To understand how this situation could have developed for Ireland, one has to go back to the simple activity of getting a loan from your local bank manager. Traditionally, a borrower went with trepidation to his bank manager and would pose the question, 'How do I stand for an over-draft?' And the response was often, 'You don't stand, you kneel.' Getting money out of a bank was akin to getting blood out of a stone. However, over time, the culture and thinking of banks changed with regard to the extension of credit. The eternal battle between the credit department and the sales force came to an abrupt halt with decisions on lending being excessively influenced by the need for growth.

In the good old days of the 1970s and 1980s, if you required money for a mortgage, personal loan, car or even a holiday, you would put forward a business case on the lines of how much you owed, what your income was, what other liabilities existed and whether you owned other assets. After an in-depth analysis of the request, a response, negative or positive, was forthcoming within a month. Fundamentally, a bank would take into consideration your total financial picture before they would entertain evaluating the risk attached to the repayment. The ability and willingness of a borrower to repay had always to be determined. It was not complex but sometimes it was burdensome and bureaucratic. However, when the approval came through, the customer felt satisfied. The amounts in question here were between £1,000 and £50,000.

During the 1990s, economic growth, inflation and soaring prices meant there was greater demand for liquidity and credit. An opportunity was apparent in the Irish banking system – lack of competition. Slowly but surely, branches of UK and Australian banks, including Ulster

Bank, Bank of Scotland (Ireland), National Irish Bank and others, including Barclays and KBC, that did not have branch networks but were active either directly or indirectly in major developmental or investment property transactions, appeared in the Republic. So the multiplier effect in lending was felt. Prosperity led to demands for larger loans in the mortgage and property areas. The traditional methods of evaluating risk by the two large banks, AIB and Bank of Ireland, were maintained as they had been tried and tested and the losses that had been incurred on any single transaction were small, very small by today's standards. When I left Bank of Ireland in May 2004, the single largest loan loss experienced in the group's 221-year history was €25 million. How credit standards would become diluted and people's judgment would become impaired!

During the period 1991–2007 banks found themselves satisfying the growing demands of their customers for credit. For most of this period, the two major banks employed credit systems that required requests for larger loans to go to their credit committees for approval. This process continued even though it was slow relative to the increasing demands of the customer base. The need for good credit analysis was observed.

All banks, under the guidance of the Regulator, have risk management committees. The risk management committee has experts in three principal areas: credit risk, market risk and operational risk. In addition to this, a bank has what is called the asset and liability committee (ALCO), the principal responsibility of which is to preserve and protect the balance sheet of the bank. This protection is with respect to capital and liquidity in the event of any strains, unexpected or otherwise, that might impair the bank's ability to perform.

It should have been a comfort to the shareholders, employees and customers to know that a strong defence in the form of robust and vigilant risk management and ALCO committees were ever present in the banks. While markets around the world became more and more complex with the introduction of sophisticated products such as derivatives, credit default swaps, collateralized debt obligations and structured investment vehicles, these instruments had little direct effect on the performance of the Irish banks and on their balance sheets.

In the early part of the twenty-first century, one bank in the marketplace had developed a very simple process for evaluating risk. Business plans and individual projects could be evaluated and credit approvals granted in the shortest turnaround time for an approval in the market-place – twenty-four hours. This organisation was Anglo Irish Bank.

It was not lost on Anglo Irish Bank that the speed of a bank's decision making often influenced the borrower's choice of bank. The principle behind Anglo's method was that the lender knew their customers, the customers were trustworthy and they understood their business better than the bank (while the bank presumably understood banking better than its customers). Each individual project was considered on a stand-alone basis. A new project in Dublin 4 was not deemed to have any relevance to a project that the same borrower might have started some twelve months earlier in Galway or Cork. If the borrower provided a personal guarantee then there would be no need for cross guarantees from other companies within the borrower's portfolio. The concept of the customer knowing his business better than the lender has been quickly dispelled by recent experiences. In many ways this was equivalent to self-certification.

This process of credit analysis was not adopted by the two big banks in the late 1990s and early 2000s. Based on the assumption that all banks carried out the same analysis on any given property loan, debates raged within credit committees as to how Anglo could turn around a decision within twenty-four hours while the two big banks with all guns firing were taking anything from ten days to a month. In around 2004, the big banks changed their attitude and moved towards a more lax analysis and decision-making culture. The pressure to close the gap between the EPS (earnings per share) annual growth rate of the two big banks and that of Anglo Irish Bank was a major influencing factor in the growth of the commercial and developmental loan portfolios. In Figure 1 (see Appendix) one can see the accelerated growth from 2004 to 2009 of lending to the private sector by the Irish banks as a percentage of GNP. The growth in this period was over 100 per cent.

The first ever US billion dollar loan in the euromarkets was syndicated in February 1982 for the Kingdom of

Denmark. I was fortunate to have won the mandate for Citi-group in London as vice-president responsible for arranging the transaction. I can recall clearly how many of my international colleagues hailed this transaction as a milestone in the European markets. This debt raising con-cluded in New York with 113 participants in a syndicate where contributions ranged from US$5 million to US$50 million each. The deal was an unqualified success but it had its challenges. Mr Erling Christensen, permanent sec-retary for the Danish Ministry of Finance, joined me on an investor tour of the US to present the economic background and outlook for Denmark. Many small banks in the US had never before considered lending money to European sov-ereigns. Caution prevailed in all the banks, as evidenced by the number of participants; seventy to eighty of the banks lent only $5 to $10 million each. Groups of interested banks attended presentations in New York, Chicago, San Fran-cisco, Atlanta and Charlotte, North Carolina. What we managed to do for the Kingdom of Denmark was to open up a totally new market of investors for sovereign debt.

What was deemed to be a milestone in borrowing for a major European state, some twenty-five years later became normal practice in Ireland for property developers. In most other countries commercial property loans would not be made without full disclosure of the borrower's financial position, including contingent liabilities. It should be made clear that in the 1980s, whether a sovereign or corporate borrower went to the markets to raise debt, full disclosure of their total borrowings, methods of repayment and the purpose of the borrowings were spelt out. Nothing was done until the documentation was in place. The size of the loans grew with the volume of liquidity in the marketplace around the world during the 1980s and 1990s, but not as freely or as loosely as it would do in Ireland in the noughties. It would appear that our level of sophisticated lending in Ireland during the heady days of the Celtic Tiger was relegated to a handshake, a promise of repayment and what now appears to have been very weak documentation.

Over the past two years I have been approached by several developers who contributed enormously to GDP growth in Ireland over the past twenty or so years. They had been caught by the leverage trap and the liquidity crisis of the banks. No two were in exactly the same predicament but they all appeared to have what I can describe today as phantom equity – equity that was deemed to be real during the halcyon days of the property market and had now disappeared through deleveraging.

Leverage was at the heart of the problem in the Irish banking system. Leverage is best described as the amount of times you can borrow a multiple of your capital, allowing you to complete bigger and bigger transactions and pay even larger prices for property. Capital has always been a prerequisite to a loan transaction to ensure that there is sufficient support to absorb all the losses in the event of a failure to repay. Leverage has the inbuilt capacity to reduce the level of capital available to cover potential losses on any given transaction. Of course, if you live in a world where there are no losses anticipated then you need less capital to protect the lenders against losses. This applies equally to banks as well as any corporate borrowers.

Too much money was being borrowed by the banks' customers who in turn had little real capital to support their activities. In turn, the banks' own balance sheets were being swollen with increasing dependency on international wholesale borrowings from the international marketplace and not with retail deposits. There have always been safeguards in place in the running of banks' balance sheets, but one of the key ratios that was eventually overlooked, and should not have been, was the loan-to-deposit ratio. In effect, this ratio should never exceed 130:100. In other words, you can lend €130 worth of loans for every €100 deposit you have as the €30 difference can be borrowed in the professional international wholesale market. The rationale for this is that depositors' money is sticky and, in times of market instability, the wholesale funds may depart more quickly but the core deposits will stay with the bank. In the event of a run in the markets there should be standby facilities to protect the bank's balance sheets, like an overdraft, in order to replace the fleeing wholesale funds and ensure that the bank does not become illiquid. Confidence is essential in the financial markets, and loss of this creates panic.

The market in Ireland has four principal segments in property lending: developers, construction companies, residential mortgages and investment properties. There are subsets to each of these but for the purpose of this observation it is best to leave it at these four. Leverage was not the preserve of the major developers, construction companies, private investors or hedge funds. It indeed proved to be the killer disease that attacked new residential home-owners. Anyone who has been faced with a demand from a bank for a loan that has fallen into arrears for an amount of less than €1 million will know to what lengths the bank will go to get repaid. Add another three zeros to this amount and imagine the respect the borrower receives when he owes the bank €1 billion or more. This borrower has the ability to hurt the bank if they are unable or unwilling to repay. As the saying goes, if you owe the bank €1 million it is your problem; if you owe them €1 billion it is their problem.

Thanks to competition and the professed need by all quarters for it, new products were being created every week, and variations on interest rates, fixed, floating or even deferred, together with mortgages that ranged from 90 per cent to 100 per cent, spurred things on. The 100 per cent mortgage was not a homespun invention, but was a concept imported into the heated residential market in 2004 by First Active, a subsidiary of Ulster Bank. We were not slow to follow and most banks allocated a percentage of their mortgage lending to this product area. It is easy after the fact to rebuke those institutions that participated in 100 per cent mortgages as there is no surer way of creating a negative equity trap for home buyers in the event of an economic downturn. Where was the Regulator at this time? Why was no action taken to curb this trend?

If a deal sounds too good to be true, it usually is. No young person or couple deserves to be trapped for an indefinite period with the fear of being unable to repay their mortgage. We now must find a way out of this dilemma, not only for those who may be trapped now but for the next generation. Homeownership is high on the Irish social agenda and, with the pains of negative equity evident in our society, the pros and cons of renting versus homeownership will have to be played out again. Finding a way out of negative equity for those who are trapped will likely benefit the whole residential market as it will remove the fear of a massive overhang in the market for first-time buyers.

Could the lenders have avoided the situation and protected the borrowers? The old adage 'know your customer' was never more applicable. The judgment of the banks was thrown out the window and unfortunately everyone – families, bankers and shareholders – have paid the price. Leverage in property must be controlled in a way that both borrowers and lenders understand the consequences of a downturn and the financial responsibility of each party in this event. Banks should be forced to recalculate what a borrower owes after a downturn. In other words, no bank should lend more than 85 per cent of the value of a property; if it does, it should be held responsible for everything in excess of the 85 per cent should the borrower be unable to repay. This would automatically transfer the burden to the banks and, in turn, would protect the customer. Banks should have strict ratios to guide them on individual mortgages and if they exceed these limits then they should absorb any future losses that might occur due to the excess provided. This would put the responsibility back on to the shoulders of the lenders and within a framework that would facilitate homeownership but would not encourage multiple unit ownership.

The effects of reckless lending on the individual might be best illustrated by the case of Caroline McCann. Mother-of-two Caroline McCann, a resident of Mullaghmatt, Co. Monaghan with its 300 mainly social housing units and a self-confessed alcoholic, failed to repay €18,063.09 to Monaghan Credit Union. Over ten years had elapsed from the time of the first credit advance by the credit union to June 2009 when Judge Laffoy made her landmark ruling. The money was long gone and McCann's memory was void of any benefit received. The fear that this mother would be separated from her children was all that remained. How any person in McCann's position could have ever raised such a large sum from a credit union begs the questions: How much was the principal? How much interest accrued? And what penalty charges were involved?

While the sanction of prison was aimed at debtors who would not pay, it also struck at those who could not. The judge found it inexplicable how the state could countenance the continuance of such a defective scheme of debt enforcement. In response, the Government moved quickly to produce a new Enforcement of Court Order, a bill which contained most of what was judged to be lacking in the previous regime.

Major borrowers now incapable of repaying their debts in full, debts which collectively run into tens of billions, are likely to be discussing their unfortunate circumstances (loss of fortune, loss of security, loss of helicopters, loss of mansions in the South of France, and so on). However, we have to thank the judiciary for their astute analysis, comprehension and swift decision making to change the system to protect the more vulnerable.

CHAPTER 3

The Culture of Silent Dissent

One of the main causes, or at least incubators, of the banking crisis was, I believe, the culture of silent dissent in our corporations and Government. Most people who have served on a board in any corporation or organisation in Ireland will be familiar with this disease. Perhaps it is also this culture that will prove to be a barrier to Ireland's financial recovery.

In the world of banking the shareholders' principal representatives are the non-executive directors on the boards of the main banks. The boards, whose principal responsibility is that of governance of the institution, are particularly charged with agreeing the strategy of the entity and ensuring that the executive management does not stray off the agreed path. Regular board meetings facilitate the reporting of performance from the executive directors together with confirmation of the entity's direction. In addition to the board meetings, there are a series of sub-committees that deal with risk, audit and compensation, and meet several times a quarter.

In Ireland there is frequently an outcry against cronyism with respect to the appointment of board members, cronyism being 'the appointment of friends and associates to positions of authority, without proper regard to their qualifications'.[14] It is also described as 'a partiality to long-standing friends demonstrated by appointing them to positions of authority regardless of their qualifications. Hence cronyism is contrary in practice and principle to meritocracy. In the private sector it would often be referred to as an old boys' club or a golden circle.'[15]

Meritocracy, on the other hand, is a system in which advancement is based on individual ability or achievement, whereby candidates are chosen for their superior talents, intellect or experience and not because of birth, wealth or privilege.

In the Irish corporate context an argument can be made both for and against cronyism. The country is small with a population that can be brought together under various ceilings during the course of life. It may well be the fact that you are born and raised in an area where you establish friendships from early childhood. Perhaps you go to the same school or university as these people and during this time you compete with them in sporting activities. The bonds that are established at birth through family relationships provide a solid basis for judging an individual's qualities of honesty, integrity, intelligence and talent. These relationships are strengthened or expanded over the years when people enter professions or build their own businesses or inter-marry. To dismiss people because of acquaintance as candidates for key positions would be foolish.

On the other hand, the case for going down the meritocracy route is simple. Choosing people who have demonstrated that they have the appropriate experience and skills for a post is perfectly fine. However, the assessment is not just about the intelligence quotient of a candidate but the emotional quotient. The emotional quotient is a nice way of indicating whether the right chemistry would exist between the candidate and the board. My own experience on international boards in the UK, the US, Australia and New Zealand has led me to believe that, when common sense combines with tried and tested processes of identification and election of directors, the results are above criticism.

Boards are often criticised for the levels of cronyism that prevail. It is because of this criticism that we need to examine what level of cronyism is appropriate. In normal circumstances, board members of public companies should have three fundamental qualities – a recognised skill base, experience in an appropriate field that can demonstrate the use of this skill base and, finally, sufficient time to spend uninterrupted in the pursuit of good governance. Taking this as a guideline, we cannot dismiss a candidate simply because we know him or her socially. However, it is essential that when that person comes onto the board that his or her independence of opinion is permitted to prevail.

Intimacy at board level often stifles much-needed debate on subjects that will determine the well-being of companies. When friends are part of an elite group it is often deemed disloyal if one professes an opinion that is contrary to accepted orthodoxies. This is the culture of silent dissent that has evolved in Ireland. In practice, silent dissent can be observed when individuals on a board or in a group disagree with policies and say nothing, disagree with actions or solutions in a given situation and stay quiet or, in certain situations, simply don't reveal their position at all. There are invariably subjects that are sacrosanct, orthodoxies that, it is perceived, ought not to be challenged or social issues that are best not talked about. Rather than challenging the status quo openly at board meetings, members of boards who might have different opinions on given subjects are encouraged to discuss their concerns privately with the chairperson or chief executive. These concerns may never surface at board meetings if, in the opinion of the chairperson, they might be considered inappropriate or even offensive to the long-held opinions of other board members. It is for this very reason that, according to good corporate governance, a member can only serve on a board for a maximum period of six years. Continually refreshing the personalities on boards is essential to effective governance.

It is dangerous to permit silent dissent to infiltrate the *modus operandi* of any board. The conscious suppression of people's opinions in favour of the status quo is often cited as the reason major oversights occur with catastrophic consequences. Accepted social norms and politeness alone cannot provide the basis for constructive, open debate on key issues that affect an organisation's well-being.

So, in the context of Irish corporate life, it would appear that the best way to get around this practice of silent dissent is to appoint experts from abroad onto our boards. People who fulfill the technical requirements and who have relevant experience in other countries should be sought out and appointed. This is one sure way shareholders' interests and the interests of the community at large will be protected. The abuse of power must be curtailed and regulators need to grasp the concept of public ownership and the nature of the responsibility of board members. Conflicts of interest are easily identified, provided they are brought to the attention of boards and not kept suppressed under a code of silent dissent.

This culture of suppression that has fed the crisis is not only found in the boardrooms but in every tier of our society. Whether it is in the family, the Church, the Government or clubs, it is ever present in our business and social lives. The recognition by the Secretary General of the Department of Finance in May 2010 that the department had made mistakes was surely a confirmation that silent dissent had prevailed. This does not imbue trust or confidence in the decision-making processes at the level of government.

In larger societies, silent dissent is less prevalent as it is diluted by the sheer size and distribution of the population. Open dissent and challenging the status quo can better serve society by refreshing our thinking. However, in Ireland, open dissent can threaten one's reputation, livelihood, family or other relationships. It is always an individual's choice to express an opposing opinion but the price paid may be disproportionate to the clarity gained.

Silent dissent, in a strange way, has given birth to the phenomenon of whistleblowing, which is when someone discloses illegal, immoral or illegitimate practices in an organisation to those who can take action.

Over the past twenty or so years, a great deal of public discourse has been dominated by scandals that have led to an erosion of public faith in commercial and other institutions. A proportion of this wrongdoing has come to light due to the actions of some celebrated whistleblowers. One such whistleblower was Eugene McErlean, a former group head of internal audit with AIB, who blew the whistle on overcharging and other wrongdoings at the bank, only for the Financial Regulator to ignore his evidence. Was the Regulator's inaction some sort of silent dissent?

The traditional view of the whistleblower in Ireland has been equated with that of the informer. 'Whistleblower' is

a term with negative connotations arising from Ireland's history of political dominance by Britain. Native informers were widely perceived to have assisted the British authorities in their rule of Ireland. Informer became synonymous with 'traitor'. Ireland continues to have a culture where loyalty is valued highly, political clientelism is practised openly, elite networks are tight and the person who 'gets one over' on the State for personal gain will as often enjoy popular praise instead of censure.[16]

Traditional attitudes have modified with time and there is evidence to suggest that there is currently a ground swell of support for whistleblowing.

The Company Law Review Group, the body established by the Company Law Enforcement Act 2001 and whose recommendations for changes in Irish company law are generally enacted, was asked in early 2007 by the Minister for Finance to consider the inclusion of a whistleblower provision in the Companies Consolidation and Reform Bill 2009. The Company Law Review Group began its discussion paper on whistleblowing and company law by stating: 'One cannot say that there is any evidence of endemic failure in relation to corporate governance or its enforcement in Ireland that negatively affects the investment climate and which requires enhanced whistleblowing provisions.'[17] The statement might have been debatable when made in 2007 but it is one which would not be countenanced today.

The opposition parties have recently backed the call of the Director of Public Prosecutions James Hamilton for legislation to protect whistleblowers. A Bill to protect whistleblowers has been in existence since 1999. In 2006, the Government removed the Bill from the Dáil agenda. An updated version of the Bill was introduced in 2010.[18] It remains to be seen whether this Bill has more of a chance of becoming law. Ireland's legal elite would perhaps find it difficult to adopt the UK Public Interest Disclosure Act. This Act runs to a mere nine pages and applies to the private and public sectors in the UK. It is an example of a simple and very effective law adopted by a jurisdiction resembling Ireland's.

Are we really intent on avoiding disclosure of the unvarnished truth in our corporate lives? Making people accountable in a commercial environment is essential if the interests of the public are to be served and protected. However, any legislation protecting whistleblowers must also carry penalties for those who engage in whistle-blowing in bad faith, perhaps because of promotion disappointment in a company. The need to protect individuals and institutions from possibly vindictive accusations by employees must be kept uppermost in any enquiry. The penalties put in place must be sufficiently harsh to ensure bad faith claims are kept to a minimum. The need for a Public Interest Disclosure Act should not be diluted by arguments about the possibility of whistleblowers acting unreasonably and in bad faith.

'That's the way we always did business, so what's wrong with it?' This is the mantra anyone attempting to change the culture of corporate Ireland is bound to hear. In the past, the accepted practices in corporate life in Ireland prevented people from recognising what today would be deemed as insider trading, which is using your privileged position to acquire knowledge of a company with which you are trading, thus providing an opportunity for you to gain an advantage over the general public. Slowly but surely, this mindset had to give way to improved standards of corporate governance.

From September 2008, the boards of financial institutions were faced with very difficult decisions. A number of chairpersons and CEOs acted honourably and gave way to the pressure for change. However, delays occurred and a lot of time often elapsed between the announcement of the resignation and the departure. This was a bit rich, considering that shareholders had seen close to 100 per cent of the value of their bank's market capitalisation disappear. Many directors actually held on to their positions on the grounds that they would be difficult to replace or it would be unfair to cast blame on them, even though many had served for in excess of five years. Perhaps they felt that their very presence had a stabilising effect on the sinking ship.

It is interesting to observe that, when problems surfaced at Royal Bank of Scotland in June 2008, they were met by the immediate departure of seven directors. The response was swift and the honourable thing was done. Perhaps we should have taken guidance from this example. It is difficult to grasp who the boards are serving when the values of shares are plummeting and many of the shareholders are being hit. Should the decision be pushed into the Regulator's hands or the hands of the new shareholders? Voting for the reappointment of directors is now an annual requirement in the UK. This will only be as effective as the commitment of the major shareholders to taking a genuine interest in the performance of directors. Ticking a box on a form is not the equivalent of having made an informed decision.

As far back as 3 June 2003, in a speech at the International Monetary Conference in Berlin, Howard Davies, then chairman of the UK Financial Services Authority, provided guidance with regard to corporate governance of financial institutions. Irish boards would do well to adopt his principles:[19]

...[P]eople are more important than processes. Many of the failed firms, or near-failed firms, had boards with the pre-scribed mix of executives and non-executives, with socially acceptable levels of diversity, with directors appointed through impeccably independent processes; yet the individuals concerned were either not skilled enough for, or not temperamentally suited to, the challenging role that came to be required when the business ran into difficulty.

...[T]here are some good practice processes worth having. Properly constituted audit committees and risk committees can play an important role, as long as they are prepared to listen carefully to sources of advice from outside the firm.

...A regulatory regime built on senior management responsi-bilities is absolutely essential. In some of the cases we have wrestled with, senior management did not consider them-selves to be responsible for the control environment and... were able to successfully claim they were not responsible even if the business failed. So our regulation is built on a care-fully articulated set of responsibilities up and down the business....We do not expect the CEO to check the bottom drawers of each of his traders for unbooked deal tickets. But we do expect the CEO to ensure that there is a risk manage-ment structure and control framework throughout the business which ought to identify aberrant behaviour or at least prevent it going unchecked for any length of time.

...[R]egulators must focus attention on the top level of man-agement in the firm. For the major firms...our supervisors [must] have direct access to the board and...present to the board their own unvarnished view of the risks the firm is running and of how good the control systems are by compar-ison with the best of breed in their sector....

...Boards should take more interest in the nature of the incen-tive structure within their organisation. I am talking about ensuring that the incentives with the firm, and pay is a very powerful one, are aligned with its risk appetite...

...[There must be] engagement on the part of the share-holders...if those shareholders are not prepared to vote and show little interest in business strategy, then that accounta-bility is somewhat notional and unlikely to be effective... Regulators cannot hope to substitute for concerned and chal-lenging shareholders, though in some senses they may complement them.

Looking at these points of governance in the context of what has arisen over the past several years in the Irish financial sector can highlight where our system may have failed.

On this subject it is worth differentiating between the roles and responsibilities of the executive and non-executive directors. The executive directors who are on the boards of Irish banks are given the mandate to manage the performance of their bank, including the protection of the bank's balance sheet. These directors are paid to ensure that the strategy of the bank is pursued in a positive way that will yield returns to the shareholders in line with market expectations. This group is ultimately responsible for the bank's survival. The non-executive directors, on the other hand, provide a strong governance framework that ensures that shareholders' interests are not put at risk. Failure by either of these groups with regard to their responsibilities requires an overhaul of the whole board. Unfortunately, the price of putting the bank's reputation ahead of one's personal reputation is often deemed to be too high. Those directors who believe they have done their best under the circumstances, and are unlikely to feel they have been paid enough fees in their career to warrant personal reputational damage, will act accordingly.

It is highly likely that at the beginning of the downturn the opinions of many non-executive directors in the banks differed from those of the executive directors who provided the financial forecasts. Discussions may well have taken place on the value of property, the loan-to-value ratios and ultimately the size of the haircut NAMA was going to demand. Experience, knowledge and judgment, all qualities meant to be demonstrated by the executives, were not in evidence. The executives, largely in a state of denial, unintentionally misled the boards with optimistic forecasts. This optimism of the executive directors did not increase the size of the write-offs and provisions, it merely deferred the judgment day. It may, however, have misled some shareholders who might otherwise have sold their shares. Whether or not this denial was a symptom of the culture of silent dissent, one has to believe that many of the directors believed differently but kept quiet because of the sensitivity of the share price and the market to valuations and provisions. Such denial led to announcements that the debts were less than they actually were, which must have contributed to the public shock when finally the extent of the recapitalisation of the banks emerged.

Common sense is required in these difficult times and it could be said that those who oversaw the destruction of the balance sheets of the banks are definitely not those who should be entrusted with their recovery. Appropriate sanctions have not been exercised in the banking system as those who were present at the highest levels when the crisis arose remained in their positions for some time after and many are still there today. This applies equally to the Department of Finance.

The need for strong corporate governance has been highlighted through major failures and lapses in corporations and banks over the last number of years. The failures invariably arose due to a lack of awareness among the boards of credit, market, operational or liquidity risks being taken by institutions. In considering reforms in this area, one might also include the issue of tackling conflicts of interest in financial institutions, so that raising a loan from your own bank, as people like Sean FitzPatrick have done, would be impossible, as it should be.

Drawing on lessons learned from the current financial crisis, the Basel Committee on Banking Supervision laid out 'Principles for enhancing corporate governance' to set standards for best practice in banking organisations.[20] The key areas addressed by the principles include the role of a board; the qualifications of board members and the composition of a board; the importance of an independent risk management function including a chief risk officer; the importance of monitoring risk on an ongoing firm-wide and individual entity basis; a board's oversight of the compensation systems; and, finally, a board and senior management's understanding of the bank's operational structure and risks.

The two major banks in Ireland, AIB and Bank of Ireland, have, over time, drawn up frameworks as to the policies and procedures for the operation of their respective institutions. A great deal of thought has been put into this area, and over the years these policies became better articulated and more suitable and applicable to their customers, employees, shareholders and the community at large. However, such documents are only as useful as they are put into daily practice. Somewhere along the line, smaller banks that were under the control of the Financial Regulator and that were independently audited failed to follow or comply with accepted good practice in relation to conflicts of interest and the moral hazard that exists in a community where a large majority of professional people were not only doing their day jobs, sometimes carelessly, but were actively moonlighting and had outside interests. For example, many members of the legal and accounting professions, in their own right or on behalf of their own firms, borrowed large sums for investment purposes. Over the past decade these investments were likely to have been in property. Whether such investments were part of a partnership's capital expenditure programme or part of a pension portfolio, they put the investor in an unenviable position when the downturn occurred. When the Government prepared a list of solicitors who would be deemed eligible for NAMA advisory work, many on the list presented conflict of interest issues as they owed banks substantial amounts on property loans on the one hand and, on the other hand, were being asked to represent

NAMA to prosecute people who were in a similar position to themselves.

Banks are traditionally cautious in the context of the borrowings of directors and executives. Normally, to avoid potential conflicts of interest, if members of one bank have a need to borrow they will do so from a competitor bank, and often reciprocal arrangements may exist to accommodate the directors and executives of the other bank. These borrowings would be used for mortgages, personal loans, car loans and shares. Frequently, an accommodation would be put in place to allow the executives to execute share options and subsequently share purchases. The purpose of these loans was always made clear and the size of outstanding personal borrowings was monitored closely. Directors and executives were encouraged to have a shareholding in their bank but the quantity of shares was limited to a multiple of remuneration (salary) or some amount that most would consider conservative. If there was, for whatever the reason, a failure to perform under these loan agreements, the discussions were of a private nature between the director and the facilitating bank. Thus, any potential conflicts of interest were avoided by the director's or executive's bank.

Auditors would send around a form to be signed annually as to what amount was borrowed during the year (personal loans and mortgages), what amount was outstanding at year end and, importantly, if there were any outstandings during the year. Of the four major banks that I have worked for (Citicorp/Citibank, Security Pacific,

National Australia Bank and Bank of Ireland), all had one thing in common with regard to personal borrowings – they were thoroughly evaluated and closely monitored. The philosophy in all four banks was that employees were committed full time to the bank and outside interests, investments or other directorships had to be approved by a designated director or a subcommittee of the board. The problem with lax governance is that it turns the potential problem of conflict of interest into an actual problem. The failure to disclose conflicts of interest to boards should be treated as a criminal offence.

The Large Hadron Collider (LHC) is a gigantic scientific instrument near Geneva, where it spans the border between Switzerland and France about 100 metres underground. It is a particle accelerator used by physicists to study the smallest known particles – the fundamental building blocks of all things. Physicists use the LHC to recreate the conditions they believe were present just after the Big Bang, by colliding two beams head-on at a high energy level. This massive project began in 1998. The first planned particle collisions took place on 30 March 2010. A brave new world of physics is in the process of emerging, as new knowledge of particle physics from the new accelerator will contribute to our understanding of the workings of the universe.

In 1986 the London financial markets had their own 'Big Bang', the phrase used for the deregulation of the London financial markets and the market activity expected to ensue. Deregulation included the abolition of fixed commission charges and a change from open outcry to electronic screen-based trading. The measures were taken by Thatcher's Government in order to make London financial institutions competitive with those in New York and around the world.

As a result of deregulation, for the first time in the history of the UK financial markets, brokers and market makers emerged and most were absorbed by major US commercial banks that wished to extend their financial footprint internationally in the securities business. The first acquisition was by Security Pacific, a California-based bank later taken over by Bank of America. In April 1986, as a director of Security Pacific Ltd, I had signed an agreement to take an 83 per cent share in Hoare Govett Ltd, the third largest stockbroker in the UK. Over six months later we bought a small market maker (jobber) in London.

A new company was formed called Security Pacific Hoare Govett (Holdings) Ltd. This institution was the first of a new breed of international capital market operation in London, which was created a mere twelve months previously. By the time the integration had occurred between the debt activities of Security Pacific Ltd in the euro-markets with the gilts and equity businesses of the established blue blood firm of Hoare Govett Ltd, the new entity had a total staff count in excess of 3,700. These were exciting times in the markets and it was not long before new premises were occupied in the European headquarters of the group in Broadgate, London.

The aspiration of the group was to achieve a prominent position in the global international capital markets. The skill base and experience of those in charge were extensive. However, nothing was to prepare us for the meltdown that took place on Black Friday, 16 October 1987. As the equity markets headed south and the values of shares were dropping like rocks into a pond, it was difficult to get a fix on the real losses being incurred. Big Bang was now rocking the UK financial markets and it would take another week to account for the depth of the cost of the meltdown. Marking to market the various positions in both debt and equity securities, which should have been done automatically, was being challenged by all as few could believe the size of the growing losses. A manual check had to be initiated to confirm the losses being incurred. For those who were from a commercial banking background, the shock of the magnitude of the securities losses was staggering. The substantial capital of the oper-ating subsidiaries was wiped out by the accumulated losses that were going to have to be recognised immedi-ately. The parent banks were well capitalised but the recapitalisation of the subsidiaries, which was soon to take place, forced a review of the strategic plans for a global capital markets capability.

The regulators who found the risk profiles of Security Pacific Hoare Govett (Holdings) Ltd unacceptable could not discern the difference between the domestic and inter-national operations in the context of governance. The steps that could be taken to ensure that no further incidents of this nature occurred were examined immediately. The macro-economic picture was akin to the hundred-year wave. Few, if any, recognised the possibility of another collapse, which did actually occur in January 1989. Risk management, balance sheet management and less ambitious strategic thinking became the order of the day.

The effects of these two crises on the UK market weren't more than a fraction of what the current crisis has wrought over the past three years in Ireland. The need for improved and strong governance is often the cry from the regulators after the fact. Unfortunately, it would appear that the speed and complexity of the markets is such that regulators are followers and not leaders. There is no substitute for common sense and good judgment, and in the face of greed it takes very strong, balanced management to make the right decisions.

The moral to all this is that the growing of a financial services business requires experience, strong skill sets and a large capital base, with a culture of managed growth suitably governed. The consequences can be catastrophic for shareholders, employees and directors if the internal and external governance is lax. Cronyism and insider trading had prevailed extensively in the London market before Big Bang. Deregulation did dilute this, since it brought the Americans in. Taking advantage of privileged information before the market was made aware was not tolerated in this new environment. The response from those who could no longer engage in insider trading was a forlorn 'How are you expected to make money?'

CHAPTER 4

Who Pays the Piper?
The Concept of Fairness in Our Society

The crisis in our economy and banking system has exposed the failures of regulators, bankers, developers, politicians, auditors and solicitors, and has led to finger-pointing in the media. It is easy to understand why those who now find themselves in negative equity, without a pension or facing bankruptcy are calling for retribution. Judgment is what the senior people in banks are paid for. When this judgment is compromised or impaired for reasons of competitive pressure, insecurity or greed, it is difficult for these decision makers to demonstrate balance in their business dealings, the consequences of which are conflicts of interest and a loss of authenticity.

Impact statements are good vehicles by which victims can express the losses they have incurred, be they physical, emotional or financial, or related to dignity or privacy. But what happens when the victim is society itself? Whatever the final outcome though the judicial system, there is no punishment severe enough to cover a loss of over €24.4

billion. The damage to the country's economic and banking reputation due to the various questionable actions under- taken by some of our banks is not quantifiable. We have an international reputation for our social, cultural, economic and sporting contributions, not only in our own country but in the many countries that have welcomed our immi- grants over the years and where a strong Diaspora has been established. We have influence internationally, dispropor- tionate to our size, in the fields of education, medicine, law and social services. This reputation has been earned and not given lightly. It has now been tarnished badly by a few, who either through greed, ignorance or simply bad practice have left themselves open to a charge of misprision of treason, which is having knowledge of the principal crime (reputational damage) and concealment thereof. The inten- tion may never have existed to damage Ireland's reputation but surely ignorance is no defence, though one has to wonder whether a plea of ignorance or stupidity would put the wrongdoers in a better light.

Our society requires standards of behaviour for all those in positions of authority, which are consistent from one profession to another. We see people every day being crit- icised for what most in our community would deem to be unethical or amoral practices. Common sense lies behind such judgments. But common sense seems to be often in short supply in the context of our legal infrastructure, which is supposed to promote justice and morality in society. As someone once said, 'If morals, ethics and law coincided, it would be a coincidence.' Creating a media court that would hear the complaints of a community with the jury being the viewers might be a worthy production for RTÉ. It would be a form of reality TV show where a case for the prosecution would be made and the defendants would be given equal time for their rebuttals. *The Court of Public Opinion*, as the show might be called, would provide a forum for people to express their concerns about the weaknesses of a legal system that appears to take an excessive amount of time to adjust to our changing society. This show would not replace any judicial system but it would provide a forum for naming and shaming people or companies who are the culprits in this crisis, punishing wrongdoers and fully recognising the plight of victims.

Concerns about the effectiveness of the law in bringing wrongdoers to account can be too easily dismissed by intellectual arguments that condone white-collar crime or acts of amoral conduct by leaders. Expressions such as 'mental reservation', 'error of judgment' and 'economical with the truth' have crept into our vocabulary of recent times. These expressions can be seen to represent an intellectual tolerance for untruth and weakness.

It appears that, in Ireland, not only do wrongdoers go unpunished but they continue to receive excessive remuneration for perceived failure.

Whether in a small, closed society or in a large, open one, people have a genuine interest in the private wealth and earnings of others. The intriguing question behind this curiosity is what others have done to succeed in a given pursuit that results in what one might describe as obscene gains. Every year in many countries, the 'rich lists' of the top 100 or 500 richest people in an area or occupation are published. With the excitement of motoring through these lists, the reader's fingers start perspiring and at some point in the process pages stick to the index finger and the page is torn. This sudden sharp interruption does little to prevent the reader reaching a name he or she recognises or coming to an abrupt halt at the poorest rich person on the list. How embarrassing. How do you manage to be the last person on this privileged list?

Who makes up these lists and where does the information come from? Is it reliable? Although the entrants are aware of the weaknesses of the process, they too are prurient. It may be easy for researchers to identify some, if not all, of the assets of the published entrants, but it is highly unlikely that they can get a comprehensive understanding of the true wealth of the entrants since who is going to disclose their liabilities?

In certain sectors of society where duties are performed on an hourly basis and the payment is made at the end of the task or the end of the week, such payment for one's labour is usually described as 'wages'. The average industrial wage in Ireland in 2009 was about €700 per week (see Figure 2 in the Appendix). This figure for the average wage generally does not excite much interest, except in relation to the average size of a mortgage.

'Salary' was a term introduced in the twentieth century and was coined to differentiate between the compensation paid to white-collar employees and blue-collar workers. The implication of this categorisation was that if you received a salary you were likely to be much better off than your colleague on a wage.

Whether you receive a wage or a salary, it is highly likely that you have had the pleasure in your life of making the acquaintance of those who charge fees. As the saying goes, 'Dentists don't charge their patients; they just sidle up to them.' So we now come into this glorious group of professions who have qualifications and make their living out of charging fees: doctors, dentists, solicitors, accountants, and many other professions including brokers and investment bankers. In terms of the hierarchy of compensation, we are now discussing the top level.

What differentiates the price for a unit of labour between parties in our society? Namely, time, effort, skill, education and experience, combined with the economic equation of supply and demand. Any job that can be done by many is valued less in society than the job done by the individual who has a scarce skill set. In medicine, finance, law, photography or entertainment we see examples of uncommon skills. Often we pay fees for a service the value of which is priceless. We probably wouldn't begrudge the fees charged by an eye specialist who removes a cataract to restore or improve our sight. This applies to the whole medical profession, whether you are talking about oncologists, pediatricians, cardiologists or radiologists.

Let's look at the medical profession at one extreme and the entertainment sector at the other in terms of our attitudes to compensation for groups in our society. Those in the medical profession are well educated and continuously trained, while the time and effort put into their pursuits entail major personal and family sacrifices. We are not an egalitarian society yet but there is a school of thought that would suggest that these skilled, learned people must or should give their services to our society on what might be described as a subsidised rate. Our society is entitled to the best medical system available and it should be available to all. The financial rewards to the practitioners may not be proportionate to the high value of the service provided. However, it is believed that there is a psychological element to medical professionals' compensation. Surely, for doctors, there is emotional and psychological satisfaction involved in caring and curing. If you are fortunate to be born with the attributes that make you join that special club in our society, which is so often referred to as a 'vocation', remember that the cost of membership can be very high. The medical profession should ensure that they are not taken for granted in society.

The nature of a financial discussion is that things can be debated in terms of numbers with all other associated facets removed. However, bearing in mind that quality of life is probably high on our list of priorities, maybe we should ask ourselves what would be the outcome if certain services disappeared. If there were no doctors, or fewer, many in our society would live for a shorter time and have a much lower quality of life. The economist might surmise that this would result in smaller contributions being required for pension funds because of the reduction in life expectancy. In one fell swoop one of the single largest financial challenges facing society in the twenty-first century – the pension deficit – would be largely dealt with. On this cynical note we now turn to the entertainment sector.

The entertainment sector encompasses a wide range of skills and talents in the areas of music, arts and sports. If we say that leverage is the opium of the entrepreneur or developer, it is perhaps fair to conclude that entertainment is that of the masses. Whether we get our fix through great sporting events, music that ranges from classical to rock or the visual sensation of a Hollywood spectacular, there seems to be no end to what fans and supporters are prepared to pay. Take football stars whose genius comes at birth with the facilities of speed, strength, touch and agility or movie stars who choose a life in the public eye – both groups receive substantial, and perhaps obscene, rewards for success. Have we ever considered the speed at which we book a concert seat, buy a season ticket or make a dinner reservation compared to our casual deferral of a doctor's appointment? Or how willingly we pay the cost of a concert or a dinner in comparison to our reluctance to pay a fee to the medical profession?

The angle you might take in this discussion on compensation can depend on what your starting point is. Are you a self-made entrepreneur who has never asked nor would ever ask for assistance from society, a professional person who is independent minded and has a fee-earning capacity, or a public servant who serves our society but who might view the fairness of our world through different social lenses?

With the construction boom we experienced an employment boom which in turn fed a tax intake boom, culminating in a government spending boom. Between 2004 and 2008, the public sector grew from 270,000 employees to 320,000, an increase greater than the total employment in the banking system in Ireland, which had grown over a couple of hundred years. The incremental cost of these 50,000 additional employees, including pensions, would be close to €2.5 billion a year.[21] Who is responsible for this cost? We know the public service and its masters did not consider the consequences, but we can be sure it is the taxpayer who will pay.

People who choose to dedicate their lives to public service have an inbred belief that they are entitled to be treated in a certain way. In fact, in almost every sector of society we have burdened ourselves with the concept of entitlement. This sense of entitlement never diminishes but keeps pace with the growth of the economy. Should the economy fail to grow, the reality of dealing with the shortfall is dismissed in favour of borrowing more to pay for yesterday's foolish decisions. In contrast, the salaries of those in the private sector adjust upwards and downwards as a consequence of their own efforts and the good or bad fortune of the marketplace.

For people to believe they are entitled to a risk-free lifestyle with an income to match, followed by a secure pension, seems to be stretching the boundaries of fairness and reasonableness in society. In a competitive world we may not be entitled to anything other than the right to earn and to be treated with respect. Our Government is there to strike a balance for our community and it must find the strength to tell us all when we have spent too much and, in turn, to reduce our incomes. If this means that the welfare payments that have seen progressive increases over the past ten years need to be reduced, then so be it. This would not be inconsistent with the cuts and increased taxes that are being experienced by us all. The Government can no longer go to the international markets to borrow what is required to fill the deficit unless they are seen to be making inroads into reducing this deficit. It may take one or two generations to get back to where we were at the peak of the boom. We have an obligation to pass on to the next generation a country in better shape than that which we inherited. I imagine that, despite our efforts, whatever we pass on to the up-and-coming generation of young adults may not meet their expectations.

During a period when every level of authority would appear to have let society down, those who provide a strong ethical and moral backbone through the public service are facing losses that they were not prepared for. The natural reaction to reject government proposals in various parts of the public sector could easily be mistaken for petulance when in fact it was a reaction to brute force and ignorance in the communication process. The reaction of offended parties will always be more favourable if they are dealt with openly and honestly. What this might lead to in the public service is a prolonged disruption to services which might well have been avoided by clearer dialogue. The void that has appeared in the management of the public sector is easily filled by unions who wish to take care of their people. Whoever is paying the wages and salaries of this sector should be strong enough to exercise their responsibility as managers of their staff. No one wishes to take a step backwards in compensation, particularly if you have not contributed to the downturn; however, it is simply unfair that benchmarking is a one-directional mechanism that does not adjust to negative growth in the economy.

Compelling reading and viewing it may be, but as the dirty laundry of the elite bankers and developers in Ireland is hung out to dry in public, the question arises as to whether the excesses of these executives are excesses in the context of the industry or only in the eyes of the public. How do people, intelligent directors, arrive at the conclusion as to how executives are to be compensated for their work? The dimensions of the executive jobs are easily measured and can be compared to similar jobs in similar markets. For bankers at a certain level, it is inevitably one of the great joys to read the headlines in the newspapers announcing increased profits, and increases in earnings per share and in dividends, and to hear forecasts on future expansion and growth, perhaps in the form of international acquisitions. The skills and experience required to deliver future growth are recognised in the form of salaries, bonuses, stock options, pension contributions and so on. Like the rich list, there is a list of highest-paid corporate officers and, on examination, nothing seems extraordinary. At least not if you happen to be on the list.

In countries that seek social fairness the highest salary is considered in terms of being a multiple of the lowest or average wage. This multiple varies from industry to industry and country to country. In Holland, the salary received by the highest paid executive is four times the average wage, the lowest multiplier in Europe. This multiplier can be in the hundreds in different sectors and countries. These differences between average and top earnings can be explained by executives who believe that the payments they receive are consistent with the value brought by them to their shareholders. In my view, executives get rewarded for creating returns on the capital provided by shareholders, whether this is based on a risk-free or a highly speculative strategy.

Most shareholders in Ireland have holdings either directly or indirectly in the banks. Over the years, no matter what the performance of the institution was, it was difficult for many of these small shareholders to understand how anyone could be worth the enormous annual compensation awarded. The market is real and competition exists, and so remuneration committees, with outside help from compensation specialists, agree a contract with the executives. One might ask whether the interests of the executives should be in line with the shareholders to ensure that a conflict of interest does not exist. Experience suggests that synchronizing the objectives of both parties leads to improved performance and growth. A return on capital is often viewed by the shareholders and the boards to be the best yardstick for performance. In financial institutions, because the amount of capital required is substantial and this capital in turn is leveraged highly, the returns on capital have tended to be high historically. If executives have the opportunity of earning large rewards for their efforts, the assumption is that the salary paid is not merely for turning up at work each day. Paying people to manage these complex businesses for success carries an implied contract of reward. The implied contract is that this payment is to ensure that satisfactory performance is achieved. The definition of satisfactory is laid out by the board and arrangements are put in place to compensate for better than satisfactory performance. Performance will frequently include the achievement of both short- and long-term goals. The problem is that if the institution fails to meet its growth targets and anticipated return on equity, the executives normally pay a high price for failure: the loss of their jobs in most developed countries, not necessarily in Ireland. What other occupations in the private sector can put a country at risk through poor performance?

As taxpayers, we have discovered to our expense that systemic risk is real and creates, financially, the single largest moral hazard. If banks don't examine the total framework of risk under which they operate, the directors are either inadequate for the challenge or are careless in the belief that they will be bailed out. The built-up frustration of the public and small shareholders is palpable. How can those who have overseen the destruction of such wealth continue in their employment and be paid such outrageous amounts?

The solutions to the banking crisis and its fallout being bandied about among the chattering classes seem to have a strong socialist underpinning. I lived in Norway for several years in the late 1970s and early 1980s. On one occasion the Vice-chairman of Citicorp/Citibank visited Oslo. He mentioned that he did not fully understand the basis of socialism in the Scandinavian countries. So, at a meeting with the Governor of the Central Bank of Norway he enquired as to the practical meaning of the egalitarian concept. He asked if it would it be right to assume that if a citizen had two houses and his neighbour had none, he would keep one and give the other to his neighbour. The Governor replied, 'Quite rightly, yes.'

'And', continued the Vice-chairman, 'if you had two cars and your neighbour had none, you would keep one and give your neighbour the other?'

'Rightly so,' said the Governor.

'And what about if you had two shirts and your neighbour had none, would you give him one of your shirts?'

'Definitely not,' said the Governor.

'Why?' asked the Vice-chairman.

'I have two shirts,' replied the Governor.

The moral to the story is that it is always easy to give away something that you do not have.

As the crisis develops we hear the cry 'Let the rich pay!' resonate in the press, on TV and in general conversation everywhere, the assumption being that the rich are not the ones who have already paid the price. After all, who else can pay at the end of the day? The revenue authorities may determine that those with income in excess of €160,000 per annum are designated as wealthy while those with assets in excess of €1 million are rich; however, we live in a community where the definition of wealthy is unlikely to be recognised by those who are in that category. Such families may in reality struggle with a tight cash flow since they must account for unexpected increases in household expenses, school fees and insurance, not to mention the predicament of negative equity. We must remember that those people who have created wealth over time are the ones who, more than anyone else, have contributed to the growth and prosperity of this country. The country needs and should encourage wealth creators. With respect to the taxation and welfare systems in the country, the increased welfare benefits that are enjoyed today mostly come from the contributions from the higher paid through capital gains tax, stamp duty and increased income tax. The tax system is driven by a need to fill the coffers to pay for the unending social welfare and public sector demands that exist and may appear to many of us as excessive.

While we are spilling over with frustration and the need to find retribution for the national economic crisis, we have to take a look at ourselves in the mirror. We can point fingers and wag tongues about the banks, the developers, the regulators, but what of the Government? The same party has been re-elected for three consecutive terms. They were not put there by the opposition but by the electorate. If we wish to vent our frustration then perhaps we should question our own judgment as we got what we voted for – an example of the price of freedom of choice. This can only raise the question as to the skill sets, experience and leadership attributes that are required by government ministers and whether some new processes should be put in place in the selection of those charged with the responsibility of leading our country.

It is foolish to suggest that rich people are just lucky when in fact most of them have one thing in common – their focus on wealth creation. Take a person who has appeared on a rich list – unless this person has inherited their fortune or married well (and divorced better), we can assume that he or she has earned the money. In turn, they would have converted some of these earnings into savings and then into investments. While luck is an element in wealth creation, it is intelligence, analysis and good judgment that underpin the retention and growth of one's capital base. You are unlikely to last the pace and retain your wealth if you are not a good risk manager. The awareness of the risks has to be matched by astute decision making.

It could be true to say that society admires and respects those who amass great fortunes, while it begrudges or scorns those who are on the lower steps of the wealth creation ladder who are endeavouring to succeed financially.

Do people who succeed really care about what society thinks about them? People who have actively amassed wealth have usually had a willing partner at the right time. For some of Ireland's wealthy that was the multiplier effect of leverage, which they now know is a good servant but a very bad master. We go through continuous economic cycles and it is experience that enables wealthy people to remain so in the face of adverse downturns. For instance, the wise reduce their debts at the first signs of a downturn to enable them to take advantage of an upturn when it comes. Borrowing is the lifeblood of business and capital growth, but it is having the flexibility and judgment to reduce one's exposure at the right time that can mean the difference between success and failure. Leverage needs to be actively controlled within the parameters of good risk management.

Whatever can be gleaned from reviewing a rich list, whether it is national (Ireland or the UK), European or in a non-geographic category, there is sufficient evidence to suggest that employees of big institutions, unless privately owned by the founders, are unlikely to be on any rich list. So, where does most of the wealth go that is created by successful companies? To the shareholders, who are invariably large pension funds that redistribute these gains to their members. Shareholders want the leaders of companies to have that internal compass that directs their organisations to growth. Often senior business people can find it difficult to grasp the difference between their money and that of the shareholders. One might interpret the attitudes of some business leaders as 'What is good for me is good for my shareholders', which is, of course, putting the cart before the horse. As an employee, you are a servant of the shareholder and not the other way around.

There is a real case to be made for the right of people to desire to become rich. Using the instrument of leverage, whether in the property, stock or commodity markets, people sought to create personal wealth through investment over the past fifteen years. Blaming people for being ambitious or greedy is a waste of time and the cry for an egalitarian system is likely to fall on deaf ears. Our capitalist system may appear damaged but it is unlikely to be replaced. It will, however, be modified as the animal spirits of the market continue to be tamed somewhat by the regulators. Capitalism, like democracy, has its flaws. However, the critics of capitalism might discover that all other systems are worse.

During a time when shortages are prevalent in most areas of society, it is intriguing to browse through the lists of plenty. Understanding that the commercial retail distribution sector dominates the rich lists in Ireland, Europe and the US might help one in determining where to invest or begin a career. The property sector is represented principally by those activities where there are cash flows attached to the businesses with a strong likelihood of these flows remaining. The entertainment sector has a number of notables but only a handful of artists achieve status in financial as well as artistic terms. Oil and technology are two sectors that have given rise to wealth for enterprising and innovative people.

In the end, the creation of personal wealth comes from innovation, energy, capital and a good business plan. Capital gains are recognised by the taxman as the necessary incentive for people to create wealth through risk taking, as the tax rates are structured to benefit the entrepreneur. Wealth creation requires commitment; there is no time for sleeping as trading in investments takes full-time attention. We should recognise and celebrate the success of individuals who have improved their lot in life through their focus and energy, and some good fortune. These people have contributed more than most to the tax take in this country, and the state's coffers require a lot more of them to reduce the fiscal deficit.

National economic recovery is about the creation of wealth. Confidence, trust and liquidity are the three main ingredients for success. As the downturn slowly levels out personal wealth across the country, we will need a new generation of wealth creators to come forward. It can be argued that the NAMA gamble is very much a shared risk with the taxpayer and, if successful, only has the potential to be credited with wealth recovery and not wealth creation. It could also be said that, if NAMA succeeds, it will be a feather in the Government's cap; if it fails, all of us will feel the effects.

CHAPTER 5

Recovery – Returning to Normal

There is no returning to normal. There will be a new normal which will come about by our acceptance of economic reality. Mindsets of entitlement and great expectations should be altered according to the new economic circumstances. Getting the nation to accept the cuts and losses over the next five years will be a stern test for the Government. The Government can only borrow so much and the tax take over the foreseeable future is unlikely to return to what it was at the peak of the boom.

When we talk about the weather in this country our choice of terminology always amuses me. We don't appear to have hurricanes or tornadoes but we do have storm force winds that are capable of taking the roofs off houses, preventing aircraft from taking off or landing, sinking ships or causing the devastation of centuries-old magnificent forests. Politically it is not a good thing to admit that you were in power when the greatest fall in economic terms was recorded. However, surely when we have experienced an 11.3 per cent fall in GDP in one year,[22] which would be enough to make anyone depressed, it would be more appropriate to label our circumstances as a depression rather than a 'deep recession'. If silent dissent is the unwritten rule for boards, perhaps it has filtered into the political and media arena also. Facing up to reality might well make the electorate, the public service, the unions and the private sector come to grips with the severity of our problems. Recognising where we are and clearly defining where we wish to be within a specified time frame will give us all the sense of achievement we deserve when better times arrive. And they will arrive.

The following expression may well reflect an underlying ethos that prevails in our society: 'It is better to do nothing at all than it is to make a mistake.' This attitude must be avoided at all costs. The economic engine of the country will be driven by risk takers in conjunction with the banks that will provide the much needed liquidity. It is important that we all appreciate the financial term 'deleveraging'. This term, which is used extensively when referring to financial bubbles, is the signpost to recovery. Deleveraging is the process by which financial institutions, investors and homeowners reduce the relative size of their assets and reduce their debts with the proceeds. The process involves an implied acceptable ratio of debt to the level of assets held.

Companies and banks often take on excessive amounts of debt to finance growth. However, this leverage substantially increases a firm's risk profile because, if the leverage does not foster growth as planned, the risk can become too much for the borrower to bear. When this occurs, all the firm can do is deleverage by paying off debt. This deleveraging is viewed by savvy investors as a warning sign.

Deleveraging applies to individuals as well as to companies. The problems arise when households have to sell off assets at a loss to repay their outstanding debts. Individuals should be cautious to ensure that through this process they do not become bankrupt. Negative equity in a home can be dealt with if the owner has a cash flow, other assets and the ability to stay in their home or rent it at a viable amount to cover monthly repayments.

From a national perspective, the deleveraging process is essential to take the excess out of bubbles, but it is not a quick fix. Different sectors in the community, be they homeowners, banks, insurance companies, investors or the Government, have to absorb the losses associated with deleveraging as assets fall to their new market level. In the past, some big pension funds and insurance companies were so badly affected by property bubbles in the UK and US that it took between ten and fifteen years to create new interest in the property sector. The lesson is that it takes time to allow the effect of deleveraging to work its way through the system. A healthy property sector requires a confident and well-managed financial system.

Whatever the new normal will be, it is going to be influenced strongly by the global economy's growth rate. As an open economy, we are influenced by the exchange rates and growth in the principal markets of the UK, Europe and the US. Much hope will be placed in the export market to pull us out of our demise, but we remain hostages to renewed growth in the US, the UK and Europe.

The first euro–US dollar exchange transaction was executed between National Australia Bank and Fairfax Publishing on 1 January 1999 in Sydney, Australia. The deal was transacted at €1:$1.1740. I was fortunate enough to make the first ever trade at 4.30 a.m. (Sydney time). It was a great occasion and was televised globally on Bloomberg TV from the trading floor of National Australia Bank. I was asked if the rate struck would be held for long or if there would there be a strengthening of the euro. My reply then, as it is now, was that I intentionally do not bet against the US dollar for any extended period of time. If one looks back at the price of that first trade and observes the volatility of these currencies over the past eleven years, it is remarkable to note how the swings have gone, with €1 trading at between US$1.59 and US$0.82 over the eleven-year period from 1999, giving a spread in excess of 80 per cent. The volatility has been enormous. Due to the sovereign debt crisis it appears that the exchange rate is moving back to the original level. The markets, as we all know, are as much an art as a science, and history has proven that what goes up in the foreign exchange markets invariably comes down.

Minister for Finance Brian Lenihan, in a paper given at the MacGill Summer School 2009, made the statement that there was only one possible path to recovery and there were three elements to it.[23] First, we must have sustainable public finances; second, we must regain our competitiveness through boosting our employment and creating real jobs; and, third, we must repair our banking system. If Ireland wants to pay its way in the world and get on as a country then all these elements must be addressed.

As we have managed to catch the wave of commercial and economic progress over the past forty years, the time and circumstances are opportune for a move towards the smart economy. The national competition for the best proposals to help turn around the economy and create jobs, 'Your Country, Your Call', is taking this challenge on by providing an attractive platform for creative ideas to come forward. The winning schemes will receive capital for their national application. Building on the inherent technological skills of the Irish workforce, we can attract businesses from around the world while at the same time accommodating the entrepreneurial character who wishes to build internet-based activities from their home. Young people should be encouraged to venture out with their creative ideas and be assisted in raising capital through government- and bank-structured schemes. The tried and tested marketing programmes of the IDA and Enterprise Ireland have proven successful at attracting new businesses to Ireland with a high demand for the technically skilled. The skill base within these agencies is of the highest professional standard and has assisted many Irish companies with international growth aspirations to pursue them. The IDA and Enterprise Ireland have what is required to ignite the national recovery plan.

The principal element of a smart economy is an educated workforce. We continue to produce an abundance of well-educated, intelligent, innovative technologists, engineers, doctors and so on, but the temptation to emigrate is enormous for these people. The number of skilled people seeking opportunities in the UK, Canada, the US and Australia is growing every month and, while not yet at the levels of the early 1970s or late 1980s, the trend is clear. Major organisations that do not consciously make the home alternative attractive for graduates are contributing to the current brain drain. It is a very complex set of circumstances but we must stretch to retain our best people and, if this is not viable, we should not lose contact with them. Those who go abroad do so to get experience and improve their skill bases and could return home to provide a valuable labour pool for the country in the future.

The losses financially and materially due to the crisis may well be offset by gains that are on a different scale. If, for whatever reason, we find ourselves with time on our hands, perhaps this is one of the positive side effects of the crisis. Time, during the halcyon days, was in short supply, whether it was for one's family or oneself. Perhaps the pressure brought about by economic stress in the household is in some way reduced by improved social relationships with family and friends. The virtue of caring is strongly linked to our heritage and cannot be described in financial terms, but it is an extremely strong currency that will outlast a euro in any denomination. Perhaps this quality will be the attraction for those Irish emigrants considering a return to Ireland.

Keeping in mind that we have many objectives in the recovery phase, not least of which is basic economic growth, the demand for an experienced and skilled workforce will be paramount in the creation of the next generation of sustainable businesses. We must become best in class at whatever sectors of this smart, knowledge-based society we choose to develop. As we have proven over the years, we can compete in many fields of endeavour but we must strive to become best of breed internationally.

As discussed in Chapter 4, individual and business wealth creation is key to our recovery. In order to produce the right conditions for this to happen, the Government and the banks should focus on three things: get people out of debt, get them investing and get them back in business.

Unfortunately, recent events make it seem that we will stretch as far as we can in order to save an entity that has created a national crisis but we are less able to accommodate the weaknesses of individuals and families. If the draconian measures that existed under the old regime, which the Caroline McCann case proved influential in changing, were applied against major debtors in the current crisis, the outcry for retribution would have been satisfied. However, this law would never have been applicable to the class of major borrower who could threaten banks with failure in the event of their default. Individuals and companies that have raised billions and now declare inability to repay can rightfully claim contributory negligence on the lenders' behalf and will possibly walk away leaving the taxpayer with the bill.

In the event someone leaves an organisation for any reason connected to alleged wrongdoing, the institution is recognised as the owner of all files and computers. Giving people months to depart reeks of weakness and indecision, which can easily play into the hands of offenders. A higher level of diligence must be required from the Director of Corporate Enforcement, and if the laws have to be changed so action can be taken, then so be it.

One can be sure that the same level of leniency is not available under law to unfortunate investors who go bankrupt. In the event of defaults in business, consideration must be given to the bankruptcy laws in Ireland. At the moment, not only is the stigma attached to bankruptcy severe, but the punishment of a twelve-year recovery period is excessive in respect to default. We must align ourselves to whatever best practice is in Europe; it might not be more difficult than examining the bankruptcy laws in the UK. In a nutshell, the term that a bankrupt serves in the UK is one year before they can go back into business and have their credit record cleared. A term of twelve years exists for bankrupts here. It appears that the laws in Ireland view a bankrupt in line with a criminal. If people fail in business and in turn fail to repay their creditors, should they be burdened with such a horrendous stigma from which they are unlikely to ever recover? The penalty of bankruptcy is out of proportion to the damage. Will a variation of the action in the Caroline McCann case be witnessed over the next year or so to prevent the stigma of bankruptcy condemning some to twelve years of exclusion from business?

Should debtors get a life sentence for misfortune, greed or poor judgment? There are endless cases of negative equity and these are visible in all sectors of the community. Is there any room in the recovery equation for an amnesty or forgiveness for part of the outstanding debt? Should a generation be relegated to a life of penury and insecurity? Lenience on the part of the creditors will possibly hinder the efforts of the regulators to have the banks recapitalised at levels consistent with best practice.

It is in the interests of the state that measures are taken to alleviate some of the stresses and burdens that are weighing down the families whose biggest crime was that they wanted to be wealthy and secure. Homeownership needs to be facilitated. The law should be changed so that the home cannot be repossessed in the event of a failure to pay debts in another area. The home is the cornerstone of society and it should be protected from the greed, weakness or foolishness of borrowers and lenders alike.

The owners of the banks come in various guises, from major institutional players to retail investors, to those whose few hundred shares mean as much or more to them as the big institutional holdings of fund managers. A great deal of trust and loyalty has been lost among this constituent. The financial losses have accumulated for each category of investor and many are left wondering if they are ever going to get anything back on the shares they hold. Will the value of the shares go to zero through nationalisation or, by some great financial miracle, will they recover to €2, €5 or €10?

It has to be understood that the major shareholders in the Irish banks who were badly burnt during this crisis are unlikely ever to reinvest in the old banks. This unfortunately arises as the major investors will put their surplus funds where they deem the opportunities to be greater and the risk a lot lower. These people never saw the banks from the perspective of networks and employees but in terms of financial investments that would generate capital gains and dividends. Often these investors would look at the annual reports and would value the performance of the Irish institutions compared to the other best-performing banks in Europe. Our banks had something more than just a domestic network: they had created a financial legacy from hundreds of years of banking practice. Good banking practice. But over time they have matured into international banks that have grown organically or acquired new businesses in wholesale banking, capital markets, fund management and insurance. The investors were able to put values on the diversified sources of cash flows, which meant, from an analyst's perspective, that, even if one activity failed, three or four others would perform profitably. On those occasions when all cylinders were working in unison, the profits were substantial and the return on equity and dividends was praiseworthy.

The big investors take what might be described as a helicopter view of our banks from the perspective of investment. From that same vantage point today, looking down on the remains of these once venerable institutions, they see little life in the future unless some very hard decisions are taken about the management and strategy going forward. This is now in the hands of the Government and the EU.

While there is no doubt that the trust and confidence of shareholders and investors in the banks have been seriously shaken, the relationship between the banks' customers and local branches, the flagships of our financial infrastructure in every city, town and village in the country, have also taken a hard knock. This situation is dangerous for the whole banking system and the local branches need to work to re-establish the trust that once was inviolable.

In the middle of this financial crisis we appear to have lost sight of the 'old' shareholders. In the Irish banking context these shareholders were either domestic or international and were made up of private and institutional investors. At least that was until the Government was forced to step in, initially becoming a preference shareholder and subsequently, through conversion, becoming an ordinary shareholder. The market capitalisation of the banks was in aggregate close to €60 billion before the crisis occurred. More than 150,000 individual shareholders held billions between them, either directly or through funds. The value of the combined shareholdings in the banks today is less than 5 per cent of what they were at the peak.[24]

We can often forget that these 150,000 were family members, businessmen, farmers, professionals and pensioners. As the market value of shares started to evaporate, tens of thousands of individuals from all walks of life were hurt financially. The nest eggs that had been put aside for the rainy day had all but disappeared. Education funds for children, fees for nursing homes, cash for the new car or holidays, or just savings for a rainy day were no longer within easy reach. Worse still, the insecurity caused by this crisis has knocked the confidence out of this key sector of our community. Savers who were unlikely to be a burden on the state are now thrust into the social welfare system that they prided themselves on being able to avoid through good planning. Is consideration given to this cadre of savers in the context of them losing more than money? They have no reason to question their own self-respect or judgment; they did their piece for society and the system has let them down.

In many ways losing one's security brings on stress for the ordinary family that may manifest itself in frightening ways. This brings up the questions of the size of the holes in the pension funds and what can be done to fill them. Many of the Irish pension funds would have held substantial amounts in Irish equities. During the past three years some 70 per cent of the market value was written off. The Irish stock market index has fallen from a peak of 10,400 to below 2,700 over the past two-and-a-half years.[25]

Over recent years, a number of Irish corporations have gone to the wall, leaving their pension schemes underfunded. The trustees who were responsible for the investment of the pension funds in corporations were charged with the responsibility of taking an arm's length approach to ensure no conflicts of interest occurred that would jeopardise their predetermined investment strategy. There are many categories of funds, ranging from personal to company to institutionalised funds. Simple investment strategies were often developed where the pension funds had overriding principles of security before growth; if growth was essential then the preferred risk profile of the investment had to be stated. Speculative funds in pension funds generally represented a very small percentage of the total to be invested. Entertaining speculative opportunities, however small, tended to be under the condition that there would be only modest losses in the event of a failure.

One of the single biggest problems for Irish pension funds is the conflict that can arise when the trustees are encouraged to invest some percentage of their funds in their employer's company. The support given to one's company through investment in some part of the pension fund is laudable and, in good times, rewarding for all. Having influence in the company as a shareholder and not just as an employee allows for greater commitment to the vision of the organisation. Whatever percentage is deemed appropriate from the perspective of the maximum exposure by the company's pension fund in the company, be it 1 per cent to perhaps a maximum of 10 per cent, should be predetermined. The benefits of so investing must be analysed and judged in the context of a possible major downturn in the economy or the company. On those occasions when the trustees meet with the owners or senior management of the company, employees may be faced with the dilemma that more money out of the staff pension fund is required to be invested in the company. The conflict is terrible and the decision to invest more of the employees' pensions into their employer's business has to be taken very seriously. Depending on the make-up of the trustees, whether they include employees, pensioners, auditors, the company secretary or perhaps some senior executive of the company, the conflict begins to simmer. If further pension funds are required to be invested in the company, the purpose for the additional resources must be explained clearly to employees. The explanation may well be couched in positive terms, reflecting the growth of the company; on the other hand, there may be veiled threats as to potential job losses if the investment does not take place.

Trustees will meet and discuss at length the pros and cons of such investment opportunities but could feel constrained in speaking their minds for fear of alienating the other trustees or, God forbid, their boss on the committee with them. This suppression of different opinions is at the heart of the failure of decision making at committee level. The trade-offs are real – an employee might decide to invest to help to save the company – but eaten bread can be soon forgotten. The consequences of allowing investment levels to rise to excessive heights in this context put the income of existing pensioners and future pensioners at risk. The price of not speaking out is enormous, not just in financial terms but in terms of future human misery. Before companies go to the brink of bankruptcy employees should clearly understand the nature of their exposure. In fact, demands for additional top-ups from the pension fund, if the amount in question is over a certain agreed limit, should automatically lead to a meeting of all associated pensioners.

As banks and other companies seek ways to recapitalise their organisations during these difficult times, there is one stage of this process that must be carried out by the regulators and the pension trustees. In entities where employees are fortunate enough to have a defined benefit plan but unfortunate in that they are reminded on a regular basis of the size of the pension deficit, it is essential that the trustees as shareholders, employees and future pensioners have an active dialogue with management on recapitalisation, in particular recapitalisation that comes from the sale of key corporate assets. These key assets, by any evaluation, would have been major contributors to the cash flow of the company and in turn would be viewed as potential ways to fill the pension deficit over the coming years. In their absence, what is going to replace these streams of profits? If there is no guaranteed future income stream to be derived then some portion from the proceeds of the sale of the assets should be allocated to the pension fund. The amount to be allocated would be easily calculated as a percentage of the sale that would equate to an appropriate reduction in the pension deficit. The principle here is that those assets that generate the cash flows currently or in the future cannot just be absorbed by the system to allow those who oversaw the destruction of the capital to be given an opportunity to repeat their mistakes. If assets have to be sold in a recapitalisation process, the conservative view would be to reduce or eliminate the pension deficit before any proceeds from the sale would be used elsewhere. Employees are not just workers, working capital or unnecessary cost centres, they are the lifeblood of companies who invest more than money into their careers. The protection of the employee has to be paramount in any investment strategy being undertaken.

As the Government contemplates nationalising the banks, they are faced with the potential liability of the pension shortfalls in the banks' balance sheets. If recovery comes, as all of us wish, then we may ask what percentage of the future profits of the banks must be allocated to pension funds. That being said, what effect would action of this nature have on the overall performance of companies and their ability to attract new investors? Fundamentally, if the banks recover, will they be able to generate sufficient profits if they are forced to sell their most profitable assets at this time to generate enough capital to meet the Regulator's requirements?

Whether people benefit from personal pensions or major institutional schemes that have taken decades to build, all pensioners are viewed as either long-term investors or traders. For most people, the strategy determined to provide an annuity will take into account many, many factors. The sophistication is extraordinary. It deserves to be as it provides security for the investor for the remainder of their days. On the other hand, an individual who is administering his own fund might be lucky enough to have a good financial advisor but in many instances may only be armed with some financial periodicals and the daily busi-ness section of the newspaper. The different skills of investors in managing money are evident in terms of per-formance and results. But the question remains as to whether we should have an investing mentality or a trading one when it comes to our pension funds. It is fair to say that few people have the training or experience to be traders. In fact, most people do not have the time to be active in the markets, as this concept of trading would imply. However, it is essential for people to stay on top of their pension performance and have a Plan B in the event they observe a potential erosion in the value of their investments.

People so often abdicate the management of their pen-sions to others deemed to be better equipped for this activity. Those who have done so in the recent past would have enjoyed the pleasure of hearing the professionals tell them that they have achieved a return on investment mar-ginally above an index or, if unlucky, some percentage below an index. It is only when they tell you that the market index has dropped by some 30 per cent or more that you wake up to the fact that you are a lot poorer than you thought. Paying a fee for this report is galling, like pouring salt in the wound. If you wish to measure performance by an index perhaps you should invest in an index fund or pay the broker only a percentage of your gains when they arise and nothing if there are losses recorded. Investment strategies that encourage us to take a passive position with our funds, meaning we wait to receive a quarterly or half yearly report on the progress of our investments, should be reconsidered. However, a person might feel trapped in this situation as they might feel that at this stage in their mature life it is possibly too late to become market aware and savvy.

All the foregoing has been raised because of the enormous volatility that exists in the equity, debt, commodity, foreign exchange, derivatives and all other markets. Post-crisis, will the volatility be reduced and will our investments in banks, corporations or sovereign states be secure so that as pensioners we do not have to worry about our security? The 70+ per cent loss on the Irish stock market, the massive haircut NAMA is applying to property loans from the banks, the fall in the value of certain collectables and the enormous volatility being experienced in the foreign exchange markets give one little reason to believe that a passive investment strategy for one's funds should be adopted or depended upon.

CHAPTER 6

NAMA – The Piggy in the Middle

There was great controversy when the announcement was made with regard to the establishment of NAMA. A variety of other suggestions were put forward and debated extensively in the media. In my opinion there was no clear simple solution other than that which has been adopted. This is a variation of the Swedish model of the 1990s (see Chapter 7) and has every likelihood of success if common sense prevails in the management and execution of the declared strategy.

In line with previous incarnations of a good bank–bad bank strategy, NAMA has been created in order to cleanse the balance sheets of the banks, enable the banks to infuse liquidity into the economy and, in turn, through the injection of the liquidity, assist in the economic recovery of the country.

On 13 April 2010, Brendan McDonagh, CEO of NAMA, addressed the Joint Committee on Finance and the Public Service:

NAMA is, first and foremost, an asset management agency, established with the aim of transferring key property related exposures from the balance sheets of the participating financial institutions in return for government guaranteed securities. It will manage these loans with the aim of achieving the best possible return for the taxpayer over a 7–10 year time frame. Replacing these property related loans with government guaranteed securities will remove uncertainty about the soundness of the banks' balance sheets, provide the institutions with much-needed liquidity and make it easier for the institutions to access capital (for some) and liquidity (for all) in the international capital markets. Financial institutions cleansed of risky categories of property loans should be free to concentrate on their core business of lending to and supporting businesses and households.[26]

Mr McDonagh went on to say: 'I want to dispel any notion that NAMA is a bailout for developers. It is no such thing.'

With this as the foundation speech for NAMA we are reassured that between the board and the executive there is a group of highly skilled and tough-minded individuals. The time frame annunciated in this speech was seven to ten years and the principal constituent in this great national drama is the taxpayer. NAMA has a clear commercial mandate to recover debt from all borrowers by whatever avenues are open to it. A key objective in its pursuits is to restore the credibility of Ireland's sovereign name as a borrower.

These strong pronouncements and policies are reassuring. We are definitely going in the right direction from the start. It would be favourable before too much time passes that a NAMA scorecard is published that highlights the key result areas and objectives of the agency. We may have a misconception that NAMA is going to be a large Irish property company. To put the size of this entity into perspective, when it has received the €81 billion in assets it has contracted to take onto its balance sheet, it will be one of the largest property companies in the world, if not the largest.

Size isn't everything but it is a good starting point. A simple plan developed over time, which indicates the anticipated levels of disposals and acquisitions, would be a sure way of keeping people's feet to the fire and ensuring that the giant does not become a sleeping giant. From a market perspective, it is important that NAMA is seen to be active, and very active at that. It is easy to say that targets must not be given as this discloses too much commercial information to the market or puts too much unnecessary pressure on the board. Whatever the pressure may feel like in these circumstances, it is unlikely to be as much as what the taxpayers are feeling as their homes fall into negative equity or they face the threat of losing their jobs. The purpose of having public targets, which could also include such items as cost-to-income ratios, the anticipated costs of borrowing versus the actual, together with the number of property completions in any given period of time, would be to provide greater clarity as to the performance of NAMA. Plans for alternative use of properties might be made public to ensure that interested parties inside and outside of Ireland can participate. All in all, there will be a litany of ratios adapted by NAMA in the interests of good commercial management. Making public the frequency and form of these ratios will lead to confidence in the existence and structure of NAMA on the part of the public.

A structured investment vehicle has been put in place to facilitate specific reporting requirements for borrowing. This structure was not designed to obfuscate the transparency that is essential in the monitoring of the performance of the agency, but it may do just that. It will be a crying shame for the agency, the Government and the Regulator if this is permitted to happen. For the taxpayer to wait and see what the performance of the entity is without having something to compare it with would be worthless. It is essential that the performance of NAMA can be measured and the results continually tracked. Legally, NAMA is protected from complying with the Freedom of Information Act. One would hope that the board will not hide behind this for an indefinite period.

We have gone through endless debates on the establishment of NAMA. What alternatives might have been considered were given an airing and then put aside. We may wish to continue debating this subject but it now has a life of its own and, in hoping for the success of NAMA, perhaps the debate can be put on the backburner as we await the progress reports. We ought to trust the ECB, the International Monetary Fund (IMF) and a number of eminent economists when they say that, by 2012, the green shoots and fruits of this decision will be visible. We should not be standing idly by waiting for some cryptic message as to the progress of NAMA. Knowing the agency's goals and targets and what is achieved quarterly, half yearly and yearly would make compelling monitoring.

In the same way as taking on loans, completing unfinished projects would be worthwhile if NAMA could enter the market as a buyer. Investment in various partly funded property projects to ensure completion is achieved would provide hope for economic recovery and a jolt of confidence to us all. At the heart of the property market there would be a legitimate market maker with the skills and strength to direct activities and speed up recovery. Confidence will not return in any form unless an organised market exists and the movement of property between buyers and sellers is facilitated.

When NAMA has completed the process of issuing bonds in exchange for portfolios of loans from the banks, which will be done progressively, the question is whether the banks will invest some of this liquidity into the corporate and consumer sector in Ireland. Having received the liquidity, the banks will be obliged to protect and preserve their balance sheets in a way they failed to do over past years as there will be an obligation on them to do so, along with strong oversight by the regulators. The new capital adequacy requirements are stringent and the new capital ratios will be followed keenly by the marketplace. That may leave little room for new lending.

However, for the country to get back to an acceptable level of GDP growth, the banks have to succeed in feeding the economy with liquidity. If we examine the option of lending funds to the customer base of the banks, we need to determine which sectors are in most need of liquidity and which of these the banks would view as good risks in normal circumstances. In identifying sectors that have genuine growth potential, it is equally important that the banks don't overlend into a particular area, causing yet another sectoral credit bubble. Areas associated with exports are clearly in the sights of the lending institutions, but, as many of these are cash rich, what working capital needs would they really have at this time? In addition, the likelihood of the export sector filling in the hole created by the losses in the construction sector is remote. Consequently, the problem for the banks as they examine the risk profile of their customer base is that the riskier credits will require more liquidity than others. Caution and discipline are essential in lending but there is no substitute for good judgment on difficult but potentially profitable projects. Working capital is what is required in all sectors but the security available is likely to have been diluted over the past three years. With €81 billion taken off the balance sheets of the banks at a discount or haircut of over 50 per cent, leaving a substantial injection of liquid assets to go into the banks, we should ask ourselves into what sector would any cautious banker put more than €1 billion?

The single biggest area that requires investment is construction and property. This sector is on its knees and we all know and understand the history of this. It is this sector we all blame for the poor state we are in today. Having experienced the massive downside of the excessive losses associated with this sector, we must ask ourselves if the economy can recover to an acceptable level within a specified time frame – four to five years – without reinvesting in construction and property. The construction industry is reported to have lost over 200,000 jobs during the past couple of years and a likelihood of recovery in the sector without investment is remote.[27]

Before we condemn any sector of our economy to a period of insignificance, it is worthwhile understanding the contribution the construction sector has made to our economy and its capability of contributing to growth in the future. A case must now be made for the construction industry being restructured so that it achieves an optimum size compatible with the needs and ambitions of our country.

The Construction Industry Federation (CIF) suggests an optimum annual output of €15–€18 billion. The construction industry was a key driver of economic growth over the decade to 2007. By the end of 2007, the industry had reached a value of €38.5 billion, in excess of 21 per cent of GNP, and employed about 400,000 people (direct employment plus 40 per cent indirect employment). This was equivalent to 19 per cent of total employment.[28]

The construction industry was likely to have been ahead of the banks in terms of recognising the genuine downturn in the market; the continual denial of the banks left them behind in their understanding of the real situation. The CIF saw that an industry of this size, resulting from a concentrated period of unprecedented economic and demographic growth, had become unsustainable. A very sharp adjustment is now underway. A further decline beyond 2010, which is now almost inevitable based on current statistics, is essentially eroding the economy's long-term productivity. On current projections for construction activity, and in the absence of a major stimulus package to reinvigorate the industry, the size of the construction industry will shrink to less than €12 billion during 2010, some 30 per cent below its long-term optimum and 70 per cent below the peak of three years earlier.[29]

The industry will be operating at almost half of its optimum level by 2011. This decline has serious consequences, as is already evident in tax receipts, direct and indirect construction employment, and wider economic activity. The result will be a deeper and longer depression which will delay any recovery. From an employment perspective, the deterioration of the industry will continue to exert a major drag on the economy; employment estimates for 2010 and 2011 suggest that total employment in the industry will fall back towards 126,000 by the end of 2011, bringing it back to 1994 levels.[30]

Based on the medium-term growth needs of the economy, construction output should be in the region of €18 billion for a number of years, equivalent to 10–12 per cent of GDP.[31] If we don't have this as a goal, Ireland will continue to fall behind the rest of the EU in our accumulated capital stock.

We struggle between restitution and retribution. It is natural to feel that we have all been let down by regulators, auditors, bankers, developers, Government, brokers, and so the list goes on. However, leaving the construction industry underfunded must be the equivalent of shooting ourselves in the foot. This sector needs to be managed from a funding and investment perspective in a disciplined manner. By ring fencing those potentially good assets and providing the owners with an opportunity to complete or begin and finish project partnerships with NAMA and the banks, we have a chance of rekindling the property market and the economy. If the major developers walk away and leave a mass of unfinished projects, the consequences for the country are unimaginable.

We are now at a point in time when the only innocent participants in the crisis appear to be the board and executive of NAMA, in whose hands the recovery of the country has been fundamentally laid. We have many more moving parts in the recovery equation but none of these will have the influence and capacity to aid a speedy recovery in a sectoral context as easily as the construction sector. The relationship between this sector and NAMA or the banks might be viewed as very similar to the medieval arrangement between landlord and serf: unlikely to foster a strong working relationship between the parties to achieve the end goal of recovery. The pressure on NAMA to ensure that no favours are done or appear to be done for the developers will unfortunately widen the rift that already exists between the three parties. The Government's ambition of infusing liquidity into the banking system, which will lead to recovery in the economy, will not occur unless civil discussions are held between NAMA, the banks and the developers with the aim of getting the construction industry off its knees. Has NAMA, in its wisdom, considered the consequences should the top ten or twenty developers emigrate? Will the Government be calling them back as it did beef baron Larry Goodman in the 1980s to save the Irish meat industry? Cool heads need to be at work in order to get the best result for the country.

Let us remember that there is an outcry by various quarters in Ireland to have the Government default on the subordinated bonds that were raised by the banks. These bonds could be bought back at substantial discounts in the marketplace today by the Government. So what is good for the goose might well be good for the developers if attractive deals can be negotiated between them and NAMA. It is naïve to believe that the major developers and construction companies will not play a principal role in the revival of the property market. The sooner the contingent risks associated with the Government's funding of banks' balance sheets can be reduced or erased, the sooner our sovereign credit rating will improve.

Are the developers' coffers empty or is there hidden treasure somewhere? Aside from excessive prices paid for some wasteland in parts of Dublin, are there not substantial assets that would benefit enormously from a recovery in the economy? To re-establish confidence and trust in the asset of property must be one of the primary objectives of NAMA. Doing this without creating another bubble is essential to the stabilisation of the finances of the country.

Remembering the lesson of the Parable of the Talents, we need to invest wisely and not sit on our capital.

A veritable 'piggy in the middle', NAMA sits between the developers and the bankers. It would be folly for NAMA to make a real pig of itself by pricing the loans at a very low rate and gobbling them up. A lesson from the Swedish experience should be taken here (see Chapter 7). Being able to price the assets being taken over from the banks gives NAMA a preferential starting place. It must determine a realistic value for the loans to be acquired. The systematic creation of a portfolio of inexpensively priced assets to exaggerate the performance of NAMA will put the property industry at risk by destroying an active market-place. Perhaps if a small selection of loans were auctioned to the public, this would in turn establish a market price. If NAMA fails to create an active market it will do a major disservice to the country.

CHAPTER 7

Looking Abroad

Within the Irish market it is important that we consider the alternatives to 'too big to fail' and 'too small to save'. The actions being taken by our Government in ensuring we have a strongly capitalised banking system are not going to be much good without a clear vision of what success looks like from the perspective of all the constituents being served. Weaker institutions in any field will become the targets of acquisition by foreign entities in the future. This may not be the preferred outcome for institutions that have histories that extend over hundreds of years. Yet, it may be the price the country, the shareholders and the community will have to eventually pay to get us out from under the horrendous financial burden that we are now carrying. In terms of our approach to tackling the crisis, it is worth looking at similar situations in other countries – namely, Iceland, New Zealand and Sweden – and how these were dealt with.

THE ALL-IMPORTANT ENQUIRY – ICELAND

A more recent example of a financial bubble and one located close to our own shores was that of Iceland. The old adage 'misery loves company' might well be used in this case. The joke that did the rounds when comparing Iceland to Ireland in terms of the financial crisis was that there was only one letter and six months difference between them. Humorous as this may have sounded, it is clear after examination that the magnitude of the crisis in Iceland is in fact far greater than that in Ireland. The Special Investigation Commission (SIC) was charged with the responsibility of determining why Iceland's banking system collapsed. The SIC's review[32] covered many key reasons, which included but was not limited to the following: the growth of the banks, the weakness of the regulatory system, easy access to credit in the banks by its own shareholders, weak equity and poor liability management.

From the review undertaken in Iceland there are some interesting discoveries that those examining the Irish crisis might do well to consider. The main cause of financial failure in Iceland is attributed to the rapid growth of the banks and their size at the time of collapse. The banks' balance sheets more than quadrupled over the four years before the bubble burst. This growth was associated with both extremely poor credit management and poor credit record keeping. The policies and procedures in key administrative areas were left behind in the response to the rapid growth targets. In addition to poor credit management, the management of the balance sheets of the major banks was in a shambles. Once the liquidity crisis started in 2007, foreign deposits and short-term securitised deposits became the main sources of funding. This short-term funding was sensitive to market conditions in both availability and pricing terms. At the time of the collapse the repayment schedules for the bonds and collateralized loans were contracting to very short time frames.

The SIC concluded that the major shareholders in the largest banks had abnormally easy access to loans in these banks, apparently in their capacity as owners. On reflection, this raised the questions of whether the loans were done on an arm's length basis and whether the banks were being run in the interests of a handful of elite customers at the expense of all the shareholders and depositors. This has a great similarity with the problems behind the downfall of Anglo Irish Bank.

With regard to the capital of the banks in Iceland, the investigating commission determined that the banks' risk exposures due to funding of all shares were excessive. There were two principal culprits in the weakness of the equity: direct loans to shareholders with collateral given in the banks' own shares and forward contracts in the banks' own shares. The banks' capital ratios did not therefore reflect the real ability of the banks or of the financial system as a whole to withstand losses. Again, note the similarity with Anglo Irish Bank's activities. The SIC concluded that loans exclusively secured with collateral in an institution's own shares should be subtracted from the equity of the institution.

Finally, the Icelandic review outlined the write-downs of the loans of the banks (the haircuts). The collective value of the assets in the three big banks was reduced on average by 62 per cent. Investigations have revealed that the quality of the loan portfolios had started to erode some twelve months before the collapse of the banks and continued to erode until the collapse, even though this was not reported in the banks' financial statements. The value of the assets was adjusted downwards in November 2008 while the balance sheets of the banks at year-end 2007 and half-year 2008 reflected highly overvalued and exaggerated values. It appears that a culture of denial in the face of large losses was universal.

Putting this haircut on the value of the assets into a national context, the GDP of Iceland in 2008 was approximately IKR1,476 billion, meaning that the write-down of the assets of the financial institutions corresponded to five years' GDP. The write-down of Ireland's assets equates to about a quarter-year's GDP so I suppose we might take comfort that at least things are not as bad here as in Iceland.

In Ireland, the suggestion by the Governor of the Central Bank to have a public enquiry into the Irish financial crisis was greeted initially with partial alarm by Government. However, since then, the Government has established an enquiry. The first stage of the enquiry is the production of two reports: the first to be produced by the Governor of the Central Bank on the performance of the bank and the Financial Regulator in the context of the crisis, and the second report to be produced by Messrs Regling and

Watson, economists and independent advisors. The latter have conducted a preliminary investigation into the recent crisis in our banking system and have made recommendations as to the future management and regulation of the sector. The second stage of the enquiry is the establishment of a Statutory Commission of Investigation. Peter Nyberg, a former Finnish civil servant with an excellent pedigree in management of financial crises, has been appointed as chairman of the Commission by Minister for Finance Brian Lenihan. Nyberg's role in managing Finland's banking crisis of the early 1990s was among the reasons why he was chosen. The Minister for Finance has said that the terms of reference for the Commission will be directed by the conclusions of the two preliminary reports.

The Commission is to examine and report on systemic failures in relation to corporate strategy, governance and risk management in the Irish banking sector. There will be many broad themes examined, including the performance of individual banks and bank directors whose wrongdoings and lax practices contributed to the crisis. The performance and structure of the banking system, together with the regulatory and Central Bank systems, will be examined in detail. This will be undertaken together with an examination of the response of the relevant government departments and agencies, including the linkage between the banking crisis and overall economic management. The report from the Commission should be available by the end of 2010.

In anticipation of the outcome of the enquiry, we should look forward to revelations about our banking system covering the following and a lot more:

- The culture of compensation for executives and the consistency of this with the long-term aspirations of the institutions must be examined. The policy framework that financial institutions operate under, which includes credit management, liquidity management, capital management, and audit and compensation committees, is well documented. The question that must be answered is how well the executive management and staff observed the policy framework. The investor relations website of each of the major banks has extremely well-articulated policies and procedures that provide enormous comfort to all existing and potential shareholders. Were executives suppressed by a culture of silent dissent when it came to the difficult questions and answers on audit committees?

- The depth of market awareness within the senior ranks of the organisations dealing with debt and equity products must be revealed. What has to be tested is the experience and knowledge of the regulators in these same areas. There has been a serious void in market knowledge among the executive management of institutions and the investigating regulators.

- We should learn about the optimal structure of banks' balance sheets and how they relate to global best practice. Are all commonly used ratios adhered to? Do regulators observe anomalies in balance sheets from one year to the next?

- The nature of authority and leadership in the banks and among regulators is another key issue. Do the penalties match the crime if specific rules are not observed in practice and do the associated penalties exceed the gains in cash terms made through the breach? Do the banks' boards listen to the guidance of the Central Bank and the Regulator?

- Is stress testing undertaken and evaluated in all portfolios of assets, whether by sector, region or borrower?

- In the strategy reviews, are the fundamental business models examined closely by the boards to ensure the executives adhere to them in practice, and do the regulators comment if the banks have strayed from their declared strategies?

- Within each of the operational divisions of the banks were there clearly delegated authorities so that executives would act either independently or with referral to one or more senior people? Were these authorities monitored and were they reviewed periodically in the context of how and when they were used?

- Is there a strong ethos of governance in the banks in practice and not just in word?

- Is risk management – which covers credit, market and operational risks – well structured, with regular reports going to the CEO and the board in a bank with regard to all irregularities?

- Are the boards manned with the levels of skills and experience in the respective areas of banking and insurance that will enable them to understand if there is something amiss?

- Who is equipped to judge the competencies and performance of the regulators?

People with authority must be assessed on their ability to exercise judgment in the context of their positions. This assessment is best made initially by people close to the scene, be they internal auditors or senior executives but, in the end, regulators must be equipped to make a judgment on the competency of any individual performing under delegated authorities.

If we look at the list of constituents who were a party, directly or indirectly, to the crisis, one can only assume that the men in grey behind the above reports will be stressed beyond the norm to meet the tight schedule. The Government, ministers, regulators, civil servants, bankers, brokers, solicitors, the Law Society, investment managers, developers, borrowers, the CIF, shareholders, employees and many, many more need to be interviewed and cross-examined. The response is likely to be mixed in the context of the availability of key people to attend meetings. Getting full comprehensive feedback from the list of con-stituents, especially in a culture of silent dissent, will be a massive exercise in itself.

Is the real purpose of the Commission to discover the weaknesses in the system and take measures to ensure there is never a recurrence of a crisis like this one? While many have sought a full public enquiry, the Government insists that this process will be much shorter and less costly than a tribunal. Provided the truth is forthcoming and transparency on all aspects of the enquiry is of the highest standard, we should be satisfied. That said, we will be for-tunate if we enter 2011 with a satisfactory understanding of what was at the heart of the crisis, the steps we must take to avoid a recurrence and the guilty parties named.

IN FOREIGN HANDS – NEW ZEALAND

A country that has similar demographics to Ireland and, some might say, similar harebrained ambitions, New Zealand should be examined for the similarities between the national crisis in that country in the 1980s and our own current predicament. The crisis that affected the financial markets and the banking system in New Zealand began in 1988 as a result of reckless lending in the com-mercial property sector through a handful of investment holding companies. The majority of the loans were highly leveraged and many of the eight major borrowers simply had cross shareholdings in a variety of companies that had little substance and possibly even smaller cash flows. The cross ownership through subsidiary investment vehicles reflected the real economic value of these companies. Initially, through active trading in the shares, the market capitalisation of the traded companies grew quickly and the perception was that real value had been created. On the contrary, there was no real value created and the consequences of this reckless lending and trading led to the collapse of the New Zealand banking system. There were other peripheral activities attached, most of which had a trading element, that simply compounded the financial crisis.

The following commercial property transaction highlights the similarities between New Zealand's crisis and Ireland's. At the peak of the market a bank syndicate put a loan together for the acquisition of a premier property in the heart of Wellington for NZ$100 million. With the collapse in the market, this property was foreclosed and taken over by the syndicate. The market for commercial property had collapsed, there was no liquidity and there were very few, if any, potential acquirers with cash in existence. The property subsequently sold for NZ$29 million. That property, some twenty years later, is purported to have a value of NZ$250 million.[33]

Former Chief Executive of Bank of New Zealand Peter Thodey explained that it was important for the recovery in New Zealand for the banks to have taken a 71 per cent

haircut in the property sector in order to re-establish a realistic pricing structure in the marketplace – a salutary lesson
for all of us. This laid the foundations for confidence slowly
but surely being brought back into the market.

It is worth noting that the New Zealand experience was
a consequence of irrational lending and equity trading
activities, which contributed to the demise of the domestic
banking system. During the crisis, the Government was
forced to hand over control of the four major New
Zealand banks to Lloyds Bank (UK), National Australia
Bank, ANZ Bank (Australia and New Zealand) and
Westpac Bank (Australia). The losses associated with
property lending and trading destabilised not just the
banking industry but also the country. The price of survival was the loss of financial independence and the
creation of a foreign bank infrastructure that replaced the
domestic shareholders overnight.

One might feel comfortable that as long as the branch
network remains the same, with the same name over the
door, one's financial system is safe. Safe it may be, but how
sympathetic is it to the needs of the local market? When
annual budgets were presented to head offices in London,
Sydney or Melbourne, with requests for additional credit
facilities for agriculture, these requests often were greeted
with a steely silence. What had been viewed as a sectoral
allocation of resources by the domestic banks of New
Zealand was now seen as an international sectoral allocation from a head office perspective. Channelling resources
to the preferred sectors in the New Zealand economy was

now out of the hands of the traditional decision makers and, in part, a national economic policy was being determined outside the country.

Some twenty years have passed since the New Zealand crisis occurred and the banking system still remains in foreign hands. Having a clearly thought out national plan for the Irish financial services industry would ensure that each decision would be made in the overall context of national recovery rather than on a piecemeal basis, hence preventing foreign ownership. Such a national plan would require strong leadership and the various constituents working together on a consistent basis. The difficulties that arise between the banks as lenders, NAMA, the Regulator and the borrowers are compounded by the lack of clarity being displayed by the leadership of the country. The complexities as to who is to be considered the most important constituent in any given transaction, be it the shareholders, borrowers, lenders, policy holders, regulators or the taxpayer, causes unnecessary confusion. Each piece of the financial jigsaw has its respective position but the need for an overall plan for getting the best deal for the country, in which each constituent has its place, appears to take a secondary position to the bureaucratic process.

A BLUEPRINT FOR SUCCESS – SWEDEN

Closer to home, the handling of the Swedish property bubble of the 1990s is another example that could give us guidance as to how we might manage to extricate ourselves from the mess of our own burst bubble.

The Swedish banking crisis had its origins in the domestic commercial real estate market, as is the case in Ireland today. Rapid increases in lending fuelled the crisis; financial companies that were subsidiaries of the banks were lending to the commercial real estate market, funded by the issuance of commercial paper. A liquidity crisis arose when this source of funding dried up and financial companies reached the edge of insolvency. With a rapid expansion of credit growth in the course of five years, private borrowing grew from 85 per cent to 135 per cent of GDP. If we care to remind ourselves, in a similar time frame, the growth of credit in the Irish private sector grew from 100 per cent to 200 per cent.[34]

One of the major failures in terms of credit decisions in Sweden was that banks lent to customers, projects and geographical areas of which they did not have sufficient knowledge (sounds very familiar). A further mistake in the lending habits of the banks was that they accepted, knowingly or otherwise, high risk concentrations, not just in terms of individual companies but also in economic sectors, primarily real estate, and within particular geographical areas.

It was uncovered after the fact that the supervisory authority had not adjusted to the changing market conditions. It continued its traditional formal supervision, ensuring that reports and permits, etc. were formally correct rather than supervising the actual risks. This lack of good practice was experienced some seventeen years ago in Sweden and all we can say today is 'Déjà vu'. Lacking relevant crisis experience, the authorities in Sweden did not perceive that the 1980s could pave the way to a new financial crisis.

The first signs of a potential crisis were observed in autumn 1990. In early 1991, one of Sweden's middle-sized banks, Forsta Sparbanken, disclosed severe credit losses in real estate lending and its capital ratio fell below 8 per cent, threatening its survival.[35] The Treasury gave a credit guarantee to the bank in order to improve the bank's ability to raise funds in the market. There was no sign at this time of the systemic nature of this crisis being recognised by the authorities. This background sounds familiar in the context of events relating to Anglo Irish Bank in September 2008. However, the global financial crisis forced our decision makers to recognise the potential catastrophe of a liquidity crisis in one bank having a potential contagion effect on the whole Irish banking system.

Later in 1991, one of the larger Swedish banks, Nordbanken, disclosed large credit losses that took its capital ratio below 8 per cent.[36] The Government now gave a new guarantee and in return took a majority shareholding. In 1992, Nordbanken and Forsta Sparbanken found themselves in trouble again as credit losses in the commercial property sector were revealed. Behind the scenes, the Government decided to merge a number of the smaller savings banks under an umbrella organisation (the current Swede Bank). At the same time, the Government bought out the remaining shareholders since it believed it would be easier to restructure the company with sole ownership. When it became clear that the credit losses were bigger than expected at Nordbanken, the Government decided to create a new company, Securum (a 'bad bank'), whose sole purpose was to take control of the distressed debt. Some 25 per cent of Nordbanken's outstanding stock of credit was transferred to Securum. The comparison between Securum and NAMA is obvious.

On 9 September 1992, Gotha Bank, a major bank, went bankrupt. Real estate prices in the previous six months had continued plummeting, and the provisions and write-offs at the bank were enormous. Sweden was now in recession, and over the three-year period in question GDP fell by 6 per cent. While the country is twice the size of Ireland in population terms, we must remember that in 2009 our GDP fell by 11.3 per cent.

At the time of Gotha Bank going bankrupt the Swedish Government issued a guarantee that no counterparties to the bank would suffer losses. This meant that the Government guaranteed all forms of bank debts, not just deposits. The Government ensured that the shareholders should bear the cost and not be included in any guarantees. Two weeks later the Government expanded the guarantee to be a general guarantee for all Swedish banks. The big question was what the limits to the guarantee should be. The answer: an unlimited guarantee in order to create the best conditions possible to rebuild confidence in the financial system.

By early 1993, the Swedish Government decided to create a new agency – the Bank Support Agency. The guiding principles of this agency were:

- All banks were eligible for support.
- Support in the form of equity was more preferable than debt, as the taxpayer would benefit from the improvements in the stock price when the bank recovered.
- The Government (strongly socialist) had the express wish not to take over banks as it had no interest in socialising the industry. Only as a last resort would banks be nationalised, and if it happened it would be a temporary solution.
- All participating banks had to disclose all known and expected losses and collateral values.
- A tricky conundrum was how the Bank Support Agency should value debt and collateral. If the value was set too low, the banks would go bust. But if the value was set too high, taxpayers would risk making a bad deal. The guiding principle was to make conservative assessments rather than the opposite (perhaps NAMA could have taken a lesson here).
- The Bank Support Agency also had to determine which of the banks were worth saving from a long-term perspective.
- A law was passed that saw the creation of a board of independent judges who were deemed to have the inalienable right to decide what the fair value of the existing shareholders' equity should be. The decision could not be appealed.

All of the foregoing has a great similarity with NAMA.

So, why was the management of the Swedish banking crisis deemed a success? The Swedish Government sought and received backing from the main opposition party for the above strategies. The achievement of political consensus was probably the most important factor that aided the quick recovery in Sweden. The two entities that were formed as the good and bad banks, which were expected to last for a fifteen-year period from their creation, were done liquidating their assets after four years and they ceased to exist thereafter. This was achieved because of the speed and independence of their NAMA-equivalent vehicles in operation. They created a market and participated actively in it with the purchase and sale of assets that led to the rebuilding of confidence in the country. This confidence originated within the country but was valued externally by the international investment community.

While the crises are similar in many ways, the dimension of the Irish crisis is unfortunately far greater than Sweden's ever was. However, there are number of simple lessons to be gleaned from the Swedish crisis that have application to our own situation today. First, confidence needs to be restored rapidly. This was achieved in Sweden's financial sector and was reflected in the real economy. A prolonged lack of confidence would have delayed recovery by years. While a severe crisis can wipe out confidence, this confidence can be restored through transparency in the reporting of the extent of the losses and the magnitude of the bad loans. The Swedes divulged all aspects of the losses publicly, everyone grasped the enormity of the national problem and consequently there was a cohesive response to the Government's proposed solution. Second, it was acknowledged that someone had to take responsibility for the losses. It is important to realise that, once the crisis had occurred, the losses could not be hidden and were dealt with in a straightforward fashion. Party politics was separated from commercial realities and an acceptable framework was set up to accommodate all parties. The shareholders were not rescued. People in general had to take major cuts in living standards. Fairness, real or perceived, was served through astute and cohesive decision making.

CHAPTER 8

The Model Is Broken – A New Financial Services Landscape

At this time there is a full-blown exercise underway to rehabilitate the financial system in the country. As those responsible for this huge undertaking try to harmonise our system to an unclear European plan, we face a dilemma due to lack of vision or lack of clarity of vision.

The Government has clearly determined that, if possible, the banking system in Ireland should stay free of total nationalisation, meaning 100 per cent ownership by the state. There are two distinct reasons for this. First, experience suggests that government-run banks are less likely to be a success. This is evidenced by the lack of socialised banking throughout the developed world. The second reason is that the temptation for politicians to spend their way into office would be too easily accommodated through government-owned institutions. It is easy to put forward a case that suggests that 100 per cent state ownership might not be a bad alternative as private ownership has brought the country to its knees. A conclusion might be that anything other than private ownership could do no worse. My belief is that we should do everything to ensure that private ownership is retained in this sector for the good of the country and democracy.

Government support packages to financial institutions are influenced by a process that has been developed by the European Commission (EC). The EC oversees whether state assistance is in line with the principles of the Common Market and whether institutions require restructuring. A broad outline of the European process and how it might apply to the Irish Government bank guarantee and the recapitalisation of the banks follows.

After the Government provides assistance to an institution, the member state notifies the EC of the nature and dimension of the support. It is implied that there would be some verbal communication between the Government and the EC in advance of the announcement. The EC then determines if the support is compatible with the principles of the Common Market. As part of the EC's assessment, it examines the exit plan of the institution in terms of the support, and consideration is given to the imposition of penalties to compensate for market distortions. The institution that has received the support is required to provide a continual update on the restructuring, which may include such things as the sale of subsidiaries, withdrawal from certain businesses and likely reduction in foreign branch networks. During this period of restructuring, it is unlikely that the institution receiving the support would be permitted to acquire new businesses.

The foregoing process has had an influence on the restructuring of the banks in Ireland. It has to be repeated that the idea of looking at the restructuring plans of individual banks in the absence of a national banking plan is tempting failure. The creativity and vision of the Department of Finance has been tested during these turbulent times and, unfortunately, I believe they were found wanting in this regard. If the sole outcome of the planning of individual banks is the deferral of state ownership of the banks then this will be disastrous. Our banks, if slow to recover, will become the target of takeovers by European banks if they are viewed as viable partners and are priced cheaply. The EC assesses whether an institution that is in receipt of state aid has a long-term future and, if not, what the time frame is for its closure. This is surely the situation for Anglo Irish Bank as justification for its survival spreads thinner.

Anglo is the living embodiment of the cause of the crisis. It is difficult from most people's perspective to recognise that those who were in charge – directors and senior executives – have departed and have been replaced by a superior calibre of very experienced international bankers. But the effigy of the crisis is Anglo and the desire to burn this effigy runs very deep. To satisfy the emotional outburst of the electorate in its search for retribution, some plan has to be devised that enables Anglo to be absorbed into another entity or to have it as part of another strategy that would see it run down in a short period of time. Both of these suggestions would have a potential contagion effect on the Irish banking system and, in turn, on the sovereign rating of the country for international debt raisings.

Any precipitous actions on the future of Anglo could have, and are likely to have, dire consequences for the country's ability to borrow. Currently, the state raises funds in an orderly fashion in its own name while the banks now require hundreds of billions to be borrowed, with the guarantee of the state to keep their books in balance. The international markets view the various debt-raising activities of the banks and the state as being separate and independent for the moment. International investors have internal categories of ratings and portfolio concentration guidelines that restrict them from investing excessively in one borrower. For the moment, the market recognises the difficulties the country faces but respects the difficult decisions that have been made to turn the economy around. If all the entities in Ireland that borrow on the international markets had to be recognised as a single borrower, there would possibly be a lack of capacity in the market to satisfy the total borrowing requirements of the country.

The management of Anglo, the Government and the Regulator have all concluded that the liquidation of Anglo at this time would be prohibitively expensive. The combined losses and funding requirements might well exceed €75 billion,[37] which would have grave systemic consequences.

The plan put forward by the new executive of Anglo to separate the activities into a good bank–bad bank structure is a replica of the previous success story in Sweden in the early 1990s. There is a greater likelihood that this approach will provide the least expensive solution for the country over time, for several reasons. The single most positive outcome of this option is the creation of a new well-managed, strongly capitalised Irish financial institution that provides much needed liquidity and competition for the SME sector.

The six Irish banks are being viewed from the perspective of what needs to be done to them so they can return to their glory days: recapitalisation, the establishment of stable boards and executive management, the maintenance of risk profiles that are consistent with SME lenders, and the creation of effective governance regimes with an active regulator presiding over them. The banks lost most of their money on poor judgment in property lending, which did not recognise the mass of weaknesses in the market. The caution that will now be observed in bank lending practices will be frustrating for the credit-thirsty SME sector. By April 2010 there was a 34 per cent increase in the number of companies placed in liquidation, receivership or examinership compared with the same period the previous year.[38] Are we going to experience one of the worst years for business failures on record? At this stage it would be a fair bet.

Lest we forget, the markets are very critical of institutions that have poor prospects for growth, and substantial growth at that. In addition, the banks will want to get out from under the government guarantee as soon as possible. In order for the banks to get an improvement on their credit ratings they are going to have to produce clean balance sheets, excellent profits, growth prospects in their respective markets and no surprises in their loan portfolios. This vision of the future for the banks has to be achieved within Ireland.

The growth of the two major banks, AIB and Bank of Ireland, offshore during the 1980s and 1990s was in response to their shareholders' demands for increased growth. The banks were forced abroad due to the lack of investment opportunities in Ireland during that period. Safe havens were sought for the investment of the surplus capital of the banks that could not be invested productively at home. This expansion into the UK, the US and, later on, Poland might today be considered a blessing in disguise. The value of these offshore investments grew and, when divested, will provide a much needed capital injection into the respective banks. The sale of the offshore assets will in no way replace the massive capital shortfall created over these past two years but it will contribute to a reduction of the banks' capital deficit. However, if the major offshore assets are sold to enable the banks to strengthen their capital ratios, some of their most profitable activities will be gone. What they may gain from the sale of the assets in terms of strengthening their structure will be offset by the loss of profits for the future, as they would be making themselves less attractive propositions for domestic or foreign investors.

More than anything else the Government needs the banks to be independent and free from government support. The

€400 billion worth of creditors' guarantees needs to be erased in a short time span and not on the never-never. Ireland's sovereign credit rating is affected severely by the guarantees, and the cost of borrowing by the state is accordingly higher than it should be. The price of this guarantee ought to be borne by those who are being protected – that is, all depositors. This group of creditors should be charged some twenty-five to fifty basis points per annum to cover this insurance. The banks need to stabilise and be able to attract deposits rather than being another burden on the Government or taxpayer. An active and aggressive plan has to be put in place to relieve the Government of the cost of the guarantee programme. These grand steps can only be taken when the loan-to-deposit ratio is closer to 1:1 than it is at the moment. The wholesale element of the banks' funding will continue to be guaranteed until the banks have regained satisfactory independent credit ratings. The dependence the country has on foreign debt and deposits should not be underestimated. Prevention of the loss of domestic deposits has to be high on each bank's agenda.

So, one way to restore health to the banking system in Ireland is through the resuscitation of the major banks by enabling them to continue operating as they have done for decades. We are looking at an uphill battle for the next several years to get the banks back on their feet and our sovereign credit rating restored to its preferred AAA status. Over the past twenty years, the banks have attracted more foreign capital into them than was available domestically.

This was in both debt and equity. The shareholders' register is a good place to start looking to see what percentage of the banks was owned by international investors. At our peak, in excess of 70 per cent of the value of our major banks was owned by foreign investors. As long as the institutions were managed domestically, we were happy to say they were Irish. In fact, they were foreign-owned, but rarely did one foreign entity exceed a 10 per cent shareholding.[39]

On the debt side, when we examine the growth in lending over recent years we can see that the domestic retail deposit base of the banks did not grow in tandem with the growth of the loan portfolios of the banks. In fact, the massive growth of the banks was supported by foreign deposits from the international wholesale markets, which were at the heart of the credit bubble. There was no end to the availability of credit for lending into the property sector until the liquidity crisis occurred. Then we realised the error of our ways.

This is the scenario we are looking at if we pursue what might be described as the 'more of the same' option. However, there is no getting away from the fact that the mould of traditional banking has been broken. Perhaps it is time to look at devising a national plan for financial services that enables us to erase the errors of the past while fulfilling the need to alleviate the Government of the massive contingent risks it has taken on as a consequence of the crisis. The thinking to date has been somewhat stifled with respect to the future activities of the banks being put ahead of the interests of the Government and the country.

If we are to consider the development of a new banking model for the country then it is best that we initially identify the key imperatives that must be observed:

- The plan must comply with EU directives on national banking.
- The structure has to provide an attractive investment opportunity for both international and domestic investors.
- The government guarantee and associated contingent liabilities should be reduced substantially and preferably erased.
- The capital structure of the financial institutions should be maintained at the highest levels recommended by the ECB and the EU.
- The sale of certain bank assets to provide capital should include a review of the potential sale of the Irish banks' payments system.
- Governance and risk management systems of world-class standards must be adopted and policed.
- Competition must exist in the Irish market at acceptable levels in product choice and pricing.
- Employment levels should be maintained but not without regard for efficiency.
- Every business must become best in class, including retail banking, insurance, fund management and SME lending.
- Reputational damage has to be repaired.

Depending on what perspective one has, one can place a conscious hierarchy on the significance and importance of each of the ten imperatives. More emphasis can be given to one imperative over another, but in the end the balance between strong numerical analysis and attention to social effects has to be achieved.

Bank*	Business Activity	AIB	BOI	Anglo	IL & P	INW	EBS
Bank 1	**Retail Branches Ireland** Number of Retail Branches** (400 branches – Bank 1)	290	270	4	60	20	110 (incl. agency)
Bank 2	**Fund Management**	✓	✓	✗	✓	✗	✗
	Insurance	✓	✓	✗	✓	✗	✗
Bank 3	**International Activities & Wholesale Banking**						
	UK/NI	✓	✓	✓	✗	✓	✗
	US	✓	✗	✓	✗	✗	✗
	Poland	✓	✗	✗	✗	✗	✗
	Capital Markets	✓	✓	✗	✗	✗	✗
	Stockbroking	✓	✗	✗	✗	✗	✗
	Wholesale Banking	✓	✓	✓	✗	✗	✗
	Excess Retail Branches	✓	✓	✓	✓	✓	✓

* The banks are Allied Irish Banks (AIB), Bank of Ireland, Anglo Irish Bank, Irish Life & Permanent, Irish Nationwide and EBS Building Society.
** Sources for numbers: Investor Relations and annual reports of banks.

The table above depicts the current banking system in Ireland according to the business activities of the banks, as it stands at the end of the first quarter of 2010.

If you consider this table in terms of the headings along the side, rather than the names of the individual banks across the top, a different picture of the banking landscape emerges. Instead of looking at the six banks and considering what we can achieve through recapitalisation, merger or closure, consideration ought to be given to examining a solution in terms of banking activities. There are many variables to this matrix, but it is worth looking at a solution that satisfies the majority of the above ten imperatives by grouping the listed banks into compatible activities.

My suggestion would be the creation of three new financial services companies. Each of these companies would be viewed in the context of the ten imperatives. For ease of reference, we will name the three entities Bank 1, Bank 2 and Bank 3.

BANK 1

This institution would simply be the flagship of Irish retail banking. Of the seven hundred branches or so that form the collective network of the Irish banking system, let us for a moment select four hundred of these as the basis of Bank 1. The remainder of these branches would be moved into Bank 3.

So, Bank 1, created out of four hundred of the existing seven hundred branches, would have the mandate to perform all the traditional retail banking activities, including, but not limited to, mortgage lending, personal loans, SME lending, credit cards, payments system, sale of insurance products and private wealth management. The geographic footprint for this flagship Irish bank could be the Republic of Ireland or it could be an all-island bank. All treasury and wholesale activities would be performed within this entity as it would be a stand-alone financial entity.

You can hear the cries of lack of competition emanating from Dublin to Brussels to Berlin. But we must look at all options and the consequences of these. This should be viewed as a first step in a long-term solution.

BANK 2

This entity would be comprised of all the insurance and fund management activities that would lead to the creation of a major Irish insurance company. All the activities of risk management, distribution, manufacturing and marketing would exist in this company. Bank 1 would be a distributor of this entity's products along with a wide range of competing products from other manufacturers. This bank, insurance and fund management company would include, but not be limited to, Irish Life, Permanent TSB, New Ireland Assurance, Quinn Insurance, Bank of Ireland Asset Management, AIB Fund Management, and all other associated entities in the fields of fund management and insurance in Ireland.

BANK 3

This entity would be made up of the extended retail banking network that is left independent from Bank 1, which would be rebranded at some future date and would have close to three hundred branches. Together with the wholesale banking activities of the system and all the international banking activities and investments of the six current banks, this institution would be viewed as a diversified financial services company, something akin to either Bank of Ireland or AIB today. This company would have clear objectives and time frames for divestments to ensure that the capitalisation of the institution reached the highest standards demanded by the EU.

With this proposed structure, the country would have three new financial entities: a flagship retail bank, a major fund management and insurance company, and a diversified financial services company.

Having looked at the measures taken in Sweden in the 1990s, if we examine the imperatives associated with the proposed change to the Irish financial infrastructure and consider these in the context of the long-term survival of the banks, we may glean a better understanding of the advantages of such change. In summary, if we were to accept the vision of three new financial entities being created out of the remains of the six banks, we would manage to achieve the following:

- Two well-capitalised entities – Bank 1 and Bank 2 – that could be packaged for sale in the event that there was not sufficient domestic equity available.

- The release of the government guarantee in whole or in part would be facilitated through these measures.

- Through the sale of surplus assets from Bank 3, additional capital would be freed up and could be used to capitalise Bank 3 partially.

- Employment is a serious concern for the industry and the country. Seeking levels of efficiency for the industry would have to be carried out with an eye on the preservation of jobs – a careful balancing act.

- The whole area of governance and risk management has taken on substantive meaning since the arrival of the new Regulator. The management of risks and not just processes would be normal practice. Skill bases in all areas of risk management would be honed. Boards and subcommittees of boards would be populated with skilled and experienced directors.

- The reputational damage that has been incurred by the country as a result of weak regulation and governance needs to be repaired. The benefit of this strategy is that the villain in the financial crisis (Anglo Irish Bank) would simply disappear, and its assets, liabilities and people would be absorbed into one of the three new entities. The new banks may or may not retain their respective names (AIB and Bank of Ireland).

- Reducing the cost of borrowing for the country and the individual banks will be achieved when our sovereign rating is upgraded. This is more likely to occur when international approval is given to a national financial services plan and international investors see that our recovery is taking hold. The savings generated from the improved pricing would be measured in billions per annum.

- Finally, compliance with any ECB or EU directive would be essential. Exactly what the EU sees as the plan for European financial services and the role of each sovereign state therein is a mystery. We await its disclosure. No one imperative should be put ahead of a total solution that works for the country within an agreed time horizon.

- Competition would exist in the form of foreign banks, but if these disappear (as they have started doing) then we would miss the value of their presence in the market.

We have a relatively open market for foreign banks to enter and compete in this country. Some of these have developed strong retail networks that compete daily in the marketplace. The decision to remain in this country will be made at the respective head offices in England, Scotland, Denmark or wherever. Halifax Bank of Scotland (HBOS) has recently made the decision to close its small retail network and end its wholesale activities in Ireland, based on the size of the market, future prospects and possibly guidance from Europe that might have suggested a UK footprint (for Lloyds TSB) would serve their shareholders better. Consideration to stay or leave at this time will be high on the agendas of foreign banks, based on variations of the reasons for HBOS's decision. The withdrawal of many of these institutions in whole or in part will lead to both liquidity and credit challenges for the domestic banking system, along with the real concern of pricing competition being reduced.

In 2003, as CEO of Bank of Ireland, I made the suggestion of a merger between Bank of Ireland and AIB. I had assumed that the strategy of increasing the banks' capitalisation for financial services companies globally was well understood in Ireland. At this time, the combined market capitalisation of the banks was in the region of €25 billion. If the entities had merged, it would have been likely for a variety of reasons that this figure would have jumped to €35 billion and, with the subsequent acquisition of an English bank, the combined market capitalisation could have reached €60 billion. Complaints of lack of competition would have faded if we had achieved a top-ten status in European banking and, in hindsight, the portfolio concentration in property would not have occurred. This would have been an unintended consequence and not a premeditated attempt to reduce property exposure. I am revisiting this vision with the above model. However, judging from the reaction to my proposal in 2003, the different cultures of the banks might prove a genuine obstacle.

It would have been very valuable if, at Farmleigh in December 2008, the Government and the Department of Finance had requested the banks to put a national plan together, jointly. This plan would have been the blueprint for the financial services industry for the next decade. Instead, each of the entities under the government guarantee was requested to submit within a given time frame a plan for their respective institution. Following these six submissions would result in the aspirations of individual entities being fulfilled and would not result in the implementation of a plan for the country that would put the greater good ahead of individual preferences.

It is my belief that the Government has the power to accept and press ahead with a proposal such as that outlined in this chapter. State ownership is not a prerequisite. The Government might have the power to achieve what is considered best for the future of Irish financial services but whether it has the vision remains to be seen.

CHAPTER 9

Misery Loves Company –
Ireland and the European Union

The headquarters of Citicorp/Citibank NA was 399 Park Avenue in New York on the south-west corner of 54th Street and Park. In 1977, the bank closed a retail branch on the opposite corner of 54th St and Park. Shortly thereafter, Allied Irish Banks took occupancy of this property as their flagship for US operations. At the opening of the AIB branch, Walter Wriston, chairman and CEO of Citicorp/ Citibank, was asked if he was concerned about the arrival of new competition in America. Wriston was the doyen of banking in America, if not the world, at the time. His response was suitably measured: 'It's nice to welcome Allied Irish Banks to New York as it is good to have someone to share the losses with in this business.'[40]

Misery loves company. We are an island but we are economically attached to other members of the EU. The historical roots of the EU lie in World War II. Europeans were determined to prevent such killing and bloodshed ever happening again. Europe was split into East and West at the end of the war, setting the scene for the beginning of the forty-year Cold War. Western European nations created the Council of Europe in 1949. This was the first step towards Western cooperation. In 1951, six countries signed the Treaty of Paris with regard to the running of their heavy industries – coal and steel – under a common management. The six countries and founding members of the European Coal and Steel Community (ECSC) were West Germany, France, Italy, the Netherlands, Belgium and Luxembourg.

On 25 March 1957, building on the success of the Treaty of Paris, the six countries expanded cooperation to other economic sectors to strengthen their ties. Thus, the Treaty of Rome was signed, creating the European Economic Community (EEC) or Common Market. The idea was for people, goods and services to move freely across borders. Over the next sixteen years, a period of economic growth was experienced in Europe. In 1973, the six became nine with Denmark, Ireland and the UK formally entering the EU. As a member of the EU, Ireland has benefited over the years from EU Structural Funds, funds allocated to less developed countries in the union to help with regional and economic development.

Over the next thirty years, the EU opened its borders and membership to eighteen more countries, culminating in the signing of the Treaty of Lisbon in 2007, which came into force in December 2009. This treaty amended previous treaties and was designed to make the EU more democratic and transparent. This transparency and democracy are surely being tested as the financial crisis impinges on many

EU states that are unable to live up to the economic standards that were the requirements of admission to the EU in the first place.

If we are to take guidance from the experiences of other countries, we should hope that comparing ourselves with the most developed countries in the world would be suitable. However, considering how the current economic and financial crisis has affected Ireland, we may find comparisons with Latvia more useful.

In 2008, after years of economic success, the Latvian economy took one of the sharpest downturns of the global crisis, which saw GDP contracting by 10.5 per cent. In January 2009, Latvia experienced its worst riots since the collapse of the Soviet Union when thousands took to the streets to demonstrate their dissatisfaction about the Government's handling of the economic crisis. The Government called in the IMF and requested a bailout of €7.5 billion. Some weeks later, after a local bank, Parex Bank, was nationalised, the country's credit rating was downgraded to BB+ (junk) and shortly thereafter the Coalition Government collapsed. In December 2008, the Latvian unemployment rate stood at 7 per cent. Twelve months later the figure had risen to 22.8 per cent. This was the highest unemployment growth rate in the EU. The forecast of a further contraction of 12 per cent in the economy at the beginning of 2009 proved to be an underestimate as the economy contracted by 18 per cent in 2009.[41]

While signs of stabilisation in the Latvian economy appeared at the beginning of 2010, Moody's Investors

Service argued that 'the strengthening regional economy is supporting Latvian production and exports, while the sharp swing in the current a/c balance suggests that the country's "internal devaluation" is working. Foreign trade and the domestic currency were the key factors in turning the economy around.'[42] These are similar circumstances to Ireland but the outpouring of dissatisfaction among the people which saw the collapse of a government would be unlikely here. We seem to be better suited to voicing our concerns on Joe Duffy's *Liveline* on RTÉ radio.

The market is starting to feel the stresses of bank defaults and sovereign defaults as the volatility index rises. We don't have to look far to see the evolution of the global crisis. Europe is teetering under the weight of sovereign economic challenges in Greece, Spain, Portugal and Italy, while a recent update written by the US Government Accountability Office (GAO) throws light on economic facts that must be considered instructive about the US. According to the GAO, the US's budget deficit was equivalent to 9.9 per cent of GDP in 2009, making it the largest deficit since 1945. The GAO went on to highlight that without significant policy changes the US Government would soon face an 'unsustainable growth in debt.'[43]

The report, which was published in January 2010, goes on to state that, using reasonable assumptions, 'roughly $0.93 of every dollar of federal revenue will be spent on the major entitlement programs and net interest costs by 2020.'[44] This implies that, in less than ten years, using reasonable assumptions, there will essentially be no money left to run the US Government, since 93 per cent of all tax revenues the US Government collects will go to pay social security, Medicare, Medicaid and the interest costs on the national debt. This implies that there would be no money left over for defence, homeland security, welfare, unemployment benefits, education or anything else for the normal business of government. As of this moment US Government debt is rated AAA. Niall Ferguson, historian and professor at Harvard University, recently wrote, 'the US government debt is a safe haven the way Pearl Harbor was a safe haven in 1941.'[45]

We are forced to reflect on the global situation and to ask the simple question – how can we, as a nation and as individuals, protect ourselves financially for the foreseeable future?

Coming to grips with where Ireland is today economically and financially, we can take some comfort when highly respected international commentators have complimented our Minister for Finance for leading the way among ailing peripheral Eurozone economies in taking the harsh fiscal measures needed to regain investor confidence – slashing public servant salaries and welfare payments. The investor community initially rewarded Ireland with a reduced cost of borrowing in acknowledgement of our sacrifices. An article in the Lex column of the *Financial Times* states:

> Ireland is no saint [imagine that]. Like other peripheral economies it became uncompetitive, paying itself too much and producing too little. And unfettered bank lending and limp regulation during its property boom brought deep recession when the bubble burst. The 13 per cent contraction

in Ireland's gross domestic product since the end of 2007 is the eurozone's worst. Output could shrink 1.3 per cent this year. Furthermore, Ireland's budget deficit, at 14 per cent of GDP, is higher than Greece's...But Ireland is not in the same league as Greece: the former Celtic Tiger has a credible recovery plan. Its public debt, now at 65 per cent of output, from 25 per cent pre-crisis, is certainly more manageable than Greece's ruinous 150 per cent...As Athens forces the eurozone to confront the problem of having one currency, one central bank governor, but no single finance minister, investors should not forget that Mr Lenihan's first mover advantage is at least 18 months ahead of his peers.[46]

We may ask ourselves whether we should just surrender and renege on our debt and go back to basics. Fortunately, for the moment, we don't have to do that, but whatever steps we take as a country, once we remain in Europe, we are all going to have a reduced standard of living. We have earned a reputation over the years for being honourable creditors and trustworthy in our dealings. Even if things got a lot worse, every avenue should be explored before a default should even be considered.

The credit analysis process appears to be the same around the world; the ability and willingness of the customer to repay under any conceivable set of circumstances is paramount. An interesting example of credit management that I experienced as head of Citicorp/Citibank in Norway in 1979–1980 was in Norske Skogindustrier ASA. This was one of Norway's largest forest product companies, which had run into difficult financial circumstances. It was a major employer and was located down the south-western side of the Oslo fjord. If the company closed down there was little likelihood of alternative employment being found in the area. The company had a mixed shareholding as it had private as well as government owners. A number of banks had extended substantial amounts of credit. These were both domestic and foreign banks, and when the company took a turn for the worse in 1980 the Norwegian Government's solution was to write off the banks' debt in the company.

For a country that prided itself in relation to the reputation it had earned in the international capital markets, the solution being suggested smacked of expropriation. At a very tense meeting of the creditors I suggested to the chairperson, a senior civil servant, that the proposed actions could be interpreted as some form of expropriation. The outraged civil servant asked if I thought I was dealing with a banana republic, to which I responded, 'I will judge you by your actions.' We had put forward an alternative proposal that would see the creditors being saved through the sale and lease back by Norske Skogindustrier ASA of a major hydro-electric plant. This proposal was duly accepted by the Government, and the financial independence and well-being of the company was secured.

The current problem of sovereign debt in Europe and beyond has in no small part to do with the power of rating agencies. Rating agencies are in the business of offering their opinion about the creditworthiness of bonds that have been issued by various kinds of entities, be they corporations, governments, banks or, most recently, the packagers of mortgages and other debt obligations. These opinions come in the form of ratings which are expressed in terms of a letter grade. The best known scale is that used by the agency Standard & Poor's, which uses AAA for the highest rated debts and AA, A, BBB and so on for a debt of descending credit quality.

It is not only investors and companies that have placed too much reliance on bond ratings. The rating agencies were first given official status by the Securities and Exchange Commission in 1975 as offering assistance to regulators to assess capital charges for broker dealers. Since then their influence has spread. Bank credit departments dropped their guard and accepted external ratings from the agencies. Slowly but surely, rating agencies extended their grip and lulled investors and institutions into a false sense of security. These agencies enjoy extraordinary protection under US securities law from investor lawsuits relating to securities they rate before they are underwritten. Currently, they are more protected than banks in the US.

Abdicating the responsibility of making your own credit assessment to an outside rating agency must surely be put in question in the future. Having recourse to your own credit analysts in the event of large credit losses must be a preferred route, as through this you can identify where the poor judgment rests. Cost will always be a factor but the responsibility still remains in-house.

The very entities that were major contributors to the subprime debt debacle in the US, with overzealous credit ratings on structured investment vehicles, are now creating a sovereign crisis of greater proportions. During a period of enormous economic difficulty, the debt-based solutions to sovereign crises are being rubbished by the rating agencies through ratings downgrades of sovereign debt in the middle of negotiations. If a state's debt is downgraded, the perceived risk of no repayment is increased, and there is a corresponding increase in interest rates on the debt. Ultimately, this means spiraling costs for sovereigns. Whether in the US, Europe or Ireland, the consequences of the increased cost of borrowing will have a negative effect on fiscal deficits, which in turn will likely lead to social unrest.

Within Europe, we recently observed the bailout of Greece. This bailout initially started with the Greeks looking for €30 billion to cover the short-term deficit the country was facing in the context of the real possibility of default. The consequences of the default of a European sovereign state had not been entertained by Brussels when the various treaties were being voted on. But in the drive for a union no one could have foreseen one of the states in an economic situation that would result in it defaulting on its foreign debt. However, today we have at least five countries in Europe that are suffering under the weight of enormous debt, and the social and political consequences for each of these countries has been – and will be – seen in demonstrations and unrest on the streets of their cities.

The interesting aspect of Greece's bailout is that it appears like a patchwork solution. Some €110 billion is being provided over two years to ensure there are sufficient funds to cover all maturing debt and interest payments. Clarity on how this massive mountain of debt was created in the first place has not been provided. It is the right of every sovereign state to borrow funds responsibly in order to balance the national books. However, Greece is a country that has borrowed in the past to satisfy consumption habits it could not afford. How much of the funds went into productive areas that would have associated cash flows to enable repayment of their borrowings? Inept treasury management has created this debacle and the brains in Brussels failed to anticipate it.

At this point Greece is facing increasing interest payments on a growing stock of debt. Athens contends that the stock of public debt will peak at 150 per cent of GDP,[47] which is likely to happen at any stage within the next two years. Many observers, including myself, would contend that this is wishful thinking. Greece faces continued economic recession for the immediate future as austerity packages take hold. A possible default by Greece has a genuine influence on the actions taken by Europe, as one has only to look at who are currently the largest creditors to Greece – Germany, France and the Netherlands. See Table 1 (Appendix) for details of the borrowings by Portugal, Italy, Greece and Spain from other European countries.

There are those who think that the IMF should have been called into Greece on a stand-alone basis. If the IMF is called into a country that is in serious economic difficulty, it will have a tried and proven method of turning an economy around. While the likelihood of this may be considered remote for Ireland, so too was the economic crisis we now face. Economic growth in countries is often dependent on borrowings, but if these funds are not used productively and sensibly the result is a financial crisis, a crisis that can only be addressed through the devaluation of the country's currency. So, first, the IMF would devalue the country's currency and so, by lowering the relative prices within the economy, would increase the competitiveness of the country's export sector and create an export-led recovery. Devaluation is also politically expedient because regaining competitiveness does not require employers to slash employees' wages, as the cost of living adjusts to the devaluations relatively discreetly. This is the hush factor.

Greece, like Ireland, does not have the option of devaluation because both countries are part of the European Monetary Union (EMU). While monetary policy is controlled by the ECB, any European sovereign entity that falls foul of the agreed economic and fiscal disciplines ultimately loses control of its own destiny. The price of loss of control translates into social unrest, be it manageable or unmanageable.

This potential Greek tragedy, while taking place some 1,500 miles from our shores, could have a tsunami affect on Ireland in terms of the precedents it could set for how European sovereign debt will be dealt with by the EU. If, in the deficit countries, the budget deficit has to be reduced to 3 per cent (in line with the Maastricht Treaty), the burden on taxpayers would be enormous, and there would be further loss of jobs and a reduced standard of living. The problems in each of the deficit European states are variations on a theme, with similar consequences of large budget deficits, rising unemployment and an outraged public. The solution for Spain, Portugal and Italy, which are suffering untold difficulties domestically, will not be achieved unless they can somehow be freed from the manacles of Europe's economic regime. Is there a chance of some form of economic easing for the offending sovereigns at this stage of the cycle? Or, in the words attributed to Marie Antoinette, should they just eat cake?

It is interesting to view the crisis from the perspective of a list of major investor countries who have been lending their surplus funds in order to accommodate fiscal deficits and soaring borrowings in other member states. Aside from Ireland, the four countries in Europe that have borrowed the most are Spain, Greece, Portugal and Italy. These four countries have an aggregate exposure of almost US$1.5 trillion to their European neighbours.[48] As we take away the veils of secrecy we find that Germany is at the top of the investor league with regard to European sovereign debt, alongside France and the Netherlands (see Table 1, Appendix). At this time, Germany has an exposure to this group collectively of some US$440 billion.[49]

We are looking at this moment at a crisis of enormous economic and social proportions throughout Europe. The political will of the German electorate may be strong enough to face up to this stern economic and financial test. Someone has to pay for the overindulgence of the deficit countries and so we believe, or hope, that Germany will get the backing from its own electorate to continue bailing out profligate nations whose governments have not been called to account. Germany has gone through twenty years of reunification and the economic and social costs have been enormous, but the prize was worthwhile. If you are fortunate enough to live in a country where a surplus is created, you will definitely wonder what is going on when you're being continuously asked to prop up nations that lack the fiscal fortitude to manage their own finances. The current generation of Germans may not feel that their hard-earned wealth should be used to bail out countries that are in situations they themselves would never find themselves in. One may wonder whether this unbalanced situation can be attributed to the growing pains of a new union or if it is a stumbling block that will see its disintegration.

The concept of pouring good money after bad might yet register with the Chancellor's office in Germany. For it is only two years ago, on 18 October 2008, that Chancellor Merkel went to her parliament to seek a €500 billion bailout of toxic property debts on the German banks' balance sheets. On that occasion, the German state marked to market the portfolio of assets and put them into cold storage for ten years – a nice way out of a difficult situation if you can afford to do it. This was technically correct, I am sure, but the day of reckoning will come in due course.

Currently, the Germans are adopting a genuine partner-ship approach in order to spread the risk and the price of economic mayhem throughout the member states. If

Germany grasped the leadership role, this would most
likely lead to fractiousness among the other union members or, worse still, perhaps raise lingering doubts about
the potentially Machiavellian aspirations of Germany. If we
in this country think that such aspirations are unlikely,
perhaps we should ask Germany's closer neighbours,
though it is likely they are exercising silent dissent on this
matter. If, because of its strong economic position,
Germany is asked again and again to take charge, then
maybe she will eventually accede. Then Merkelvelli might
have achieved in one charitable move that which her pred-
ecessors failed to do by conflict. A sobering thought.

In May 2010 the financial stabilisation package that took
EU finance ministers some eleven hours to cobble together
amounted to a €750 billion facility, which was a combination of contributions from the EU, the EC and the IMF. In
broad terms, the IMF provided a 50 per cent supplement to
the €500 million agreed by the EU. These funds may be used
for the various purposes of the indebted sovereigns, but the
price of these facilities goes far beyond the level of interest
being charged. The fiscal deficits of the borrowing sovereigns will have to be reduced in line with a predetermined
plan, with scant regard for the domestic consequences in
each country.

It appears that, in the first instance, the EC, ECB, EU and
IMF condone the use of debt, even if the debt is not used for
productive purposes but to repay the amount of existing
debt. Perhaps this was the blueprint Irish developers and
banks were working from. Surely if you have to borrow

billions to pay back billions then perhaps you should not have borrowed or lent in the first instance.

One might like to ask when and how all these sovereign debts are going to be repaid. If the new borrowings by sovereigns are not put to productive use, there will be no new cash flows to repay the old debts or the new extra debt that has been taken on to defer the repayment of the old debts. A banker's dream; compound interest at its best. Who are we kidding? The need for credit for both investment and consumption is required for any expanding economy. If, however, the majority of the borrowings are used to defer the day of reckoning, we have simply created a never-ending cycle of borrowing to repay the debt on which the borrower has the potential to default, with the total debt mountain growing on each occasion. Under this scenario, better referred to as 'the deferral system of stabilisation', the sovereign borrowers are unlikely to be in a position to repay the ever-increasing core debt. A large portion of this core debt is an interest bill that could not be paid in the first instance and adds to the repayment burden of the sovereign borrower. Those who lend the money believe their investments are secure because they hold the guarantees of some perceived credible entity. If the borrowers are unable, rather than unwilling, to repay because of domestic financial issues then the guarantors, because of circumstances, may turn out to be less creditworthy.

As this relatively new phenomenon of potential sovereign debt defaults looms over Europe, we might consider looking to the emerging markets where firms like Morgan

Stanley International have had substantial experience in sovereign restructuring and defaults. The lessons learnt from the experiences of the emerging markets are worth noting as the characteristics of the challenges are common to the situations in many European states today.

First, looking at the instances of default in emerging markets from the macro-economic perspective, we note that fiscal deficits combined with recession have been prevalent features in what eventually turned out to be sovereign debt default episodes. The fiscal side of the economy has played a more influential role than government debt-to-GDP ratios. The market concern over default relates more to repayment prospects and the sustainability of the debt rather than the overall debt burden. This red flag is blowing in the financial winds over many European nations today, including Ireland.

The second element to consider is the age-old concern of credit analysts everywhere: the ability and willingness of the debtor to repay. Sovereigns in emerging markets tend to default when there is no possibility of refinancing, combined with domestic political considerations. The dimension of external versus internal constituent factors influences policy makers to retain scarce resources for domestic residents over external creditors. The option of default exists but the consequences are punishing in varying degrees. It is worth noting that, in cases of default, there was no clear evidence of the original loans being used for consumption, productive investment purposes or exotic developments of a non-commercial nature.

In the midst of restructuring due to sovereign crisis, it is common to encounter denial. Liquidity and solvency are the soul mates of more new money and extended time for repayment. The process resulting in episodes of sovereign bond defaults in emerging markets does not take a straight line from the market sensing payment duress to default. Most episodes involve policy makers denying the existence of payment duress and attempting many approaches, including outside assistance and support, before considering a restructure or movement towards default.

Sovereign defaults in emerging markets tend to happen in periodic clusters and are rarely isolated incidents. They are typically linked to boom–bust cycles, with easy credit leading to a boom in borrowing and tight credit leading to difficulties in refinancing and ultimately default. Does this sound familiar? So, hopefully, we can learn lessons from what might be described as the experiences of our less fortunate emerging market debtors and take heed of what we must consider in approaching solutions to financial turmoil in Ireland and Europe.

For the moment, let us avoid denial and recognise the dimension of the European problem. The fiscal deficits that plague many of the sovereign states in Europe need a coordinated response that pleases the investor community. Is the easing of the burden of this crisis not best served by creating a two-tier euro with the express intent of returning to one euro for all within a specified time frame? The countries that would join the second tier would be those that have failed to manage their economies in line with the

Maastricht Treaty, while Germany and France and a few more countries would share the first tier, creating a super euro. This action would permit the devaluation of the euro and at the same time a revaluation of the super euro. It would enable the countries in the second tier to devalue their euro by an agreed percentage or see the birth of a super euro which would revalue upwards. In time, the separation of the two could be bridged with a reconcilement treaty at new agreed rates of exchange. This process would recognise that the financial maturity of all member states was not equal from the outset. It would also serve the political wish to continue with the ambitions of the EU while showing a much needed flexibility in dealing with fiscal deficits. This would allow the domestic, economic and social issues within Ireland and other deficit countries to be addressed over an agreed period of time before they rejoin the EMU.

The difficulties of this proposal might be far more palatable to the electorate in all countries than the more rigid solution facing us today: reducing our budget deficits through draconian measures while limiting the borrowing of the indebted countries to more moderate levels. It is worth noting that, whatever the political costs that might be incurred, the economic and social costs would be less severe this way.

What we are experiencing as a result of the financial crisis is an ever-increasing domestic, European and global debt problem. At some point, the nations with surpluses will conclude that investing in these deficit states in the long term puts at risk the future of pension schemes, investment plans and allied welfare projects. When a country's reserves are invested in defaulting sovereign bonds, it is the taxpayer who ultimately suffers. Thus, the national reserves which were once viewed as safe may no longer be worth the IOUs they are written on. Is it any wonder the German electorate is concerned?

It is a global dilemma that may continue for some time unless the borrowers and investors sit down together to work out a solution, a solution that requires the deleveraging of the investors' assets. An unpalatable solution that might be arrived at would be an acceptance by sovereign investors (banks) that interest is not permitted to be rolled up and that any interest payments over the next three to five years goes towards the reduction of the outstanding principal. This suggestion, while giving heartburn to investors, will provide an orderly way for debtor nations to get into equilibrium with the investor community. Some twenty years ago, Russia did the unbelievable and defaulted on her debts. To no one's amazement she returned to the international capital markets this year. There has been a healing process and the patient has recovered to be a respected issuer in the markets once again.

The solutions that have worked for developing countries in the past may have every bit as much application today for developed nations that have over-borrowed and are on the verge of defaulting. Debt relief for developing countries on the part of their creditor banks was a key element of the

March 1989 Brady Plan in the US. The Brady Plan called for the US Treasury and multilateral lending agencies (including the IMF and the World Bank) to cooperate with bank creditors in restructuring and reducing the debt of those developing countries, including Mexico, that were pursuing structural adjustment and economic programmes supported by these agencies. A haircut of 30 per cent of the outstanding debt was taken and new bonds were issued to replace the bank loans.

The stigma attached to a bailout may be deemed unpalatable for developed nations experiencing debt management problems that are of their own making. If the money that has been borrowed in the past by several of the debt-ridden states in Europe has not been invested into productive projects, it is unlikely that the provision of further monies by the ECB, World Bank, IMF or whomever to assist the debtor nations from defaulting will do anything other than defer the day of reckoning. The likes of Greece have bought time, at most eighteen months. However, the Greek debt mountain has continued to grow and the ability of the country to repay its principal and interest inside the current time frame has magnified the problem.

Sovereign bailouts are far more complicated than bank bailouts. Be that as it may, there would appear to be a series of these bailouts looming in Europe unless an alternative is found that is economically acceptable at the sovereign level and politically acceptable at the European level. The EU can afford to bail out a single sovereign if it so wishes, but it would be a dangerous precedent and might leave the EU open to the burden of multiple country bailouts. The single currency is the trap that will cause the reappraisal of the viability of the EU.

A solution similar to that of NAMA could be introduced for Europe. A new European entity called SAMA (Sovereign Asset Management Agency) could be established, the principal objective of which would be to resolve the debt crisis by whatever means agreed. This entity might buy back a certain percentage of each troubled nation's maturing debt in exchange for bonds newly issued by the ECB or by the debtor nation with the guarantee of the ECB. The existing bond holders would have a lot to say about the price to be paid for the maturing debt, but these negotiations are likely to be between the surplus sovereign states and those in deficit in the EU.

Economic challenges will exist for many years to come for the member states of the EU. Whether a solution for any EU member in financial difficulty is negotiated or imposed, the need for certainty and clarity to restore confidence in the markets is a must.

CONCLUSION

Don't Waste the Crisis

From this vantage point, we can look back at where we were in Ireland some twenty years ago. Ireland emerged from the 1970s and 1980s as one of the least prosperous countries in the EU. Our income per capita compared to the rest of Europe was at the bottom of the scale. The infrastructure in the country was not up to European standards and so a national plan was put in place. The improvements that have been achieved since then are remarkable, and are a testament to the fact that not all that was invested in the country's infrastructure was a waste. One can argue that there might have been more invested and this more efficiently used. But who could have foreseen in 1990 what the country looks like today? We got ahead of ourselves, but that does not mean we should dismiss the incredible economic success of those sixteen years from 1991 to 2007. Our expectations grew faster than our ability to deliver, but we need to sit down and produce another twenty-year plan for Ireland that will bring us into a position that the next generation will be proud to inherit.

We have been the beneficiaries of the grace and favours bestowed on us as members of the EU since we joined in 1973. Our membership of Europe has to have balance in all aspects, particularly in relation to our culture, our sovereignty and the price we pay for our economic and financial independence. Have we unwittingly surrendered these precious aspects of our society as the price of EU membership? As we search for solutions to the crisis, we should pay attention to what might provide the best outcome in the long term for the country. In this context there is another option that is, I believe, worth a glance: if all else fails then perhaps we should stretch our thinking, widen our view and look west, not east.

Alaska and Hawaii are the forty-ninth and fiftieth states in the US. Both of these states are geographically and, it could be argued, culturally further away from Washington, DC than Ireland. Just for a moment let us question why our hands are tied at this time as a member of the EU. If we are in search of a solution and Europe finds it difficult to accommodate the needs of the Irish electorate, should we look elsewhere? Although because of geographic proximity we are associated with Europe, previous generations of Irish emigrants have chosen the US as their home, perhaps because we have never been strong linguistically. We have a special place in US history and society, but maybe we could take this further and become the fifty-first state. Fifty years from now, out of the new fifty-first state could come a young, ambitious Irish person with the potential to be the new President of the United States.

We might consider this option unthinkable but fifty years ago we may have thought membership of a European Union or United States of Europe to be impossible. Whatever route we take, the country has and will have to make sacrifices in the context of its sovereignty. Surrendering our independence would never be palatable but that's what we have done through our membership of the EU. This may be the wrong time to put forward a negotiated plan that could result in a form of economic and political surrender. However, if we cannot make a decision on the financial aspects of our economy without referring to the EU or the ECB then we have done just that. This being the case, if there was an alternative to the EU, should we not examine the benefits of it as well as the negative consequences? This is not an exercise in futility if such consideration would open our eyes to the advantages of being associated with the current world economic power. In this time of crisis, every avenue open to us as regards our recovery and associated dependencies must at least be entertained. The possible consequences of political and economic association with the US would be a massive influx of foreign direct investment, a link to the US dollar, a reduction in unemployment and, who knows, maybe an annual payment for a number of years to get our finances back in balance. Of course, there are obvious downsides to this route, including the massive disapproval of our closest neighbours. In any case, our advances could easily be met with rejection by Uncle Sam. While, politically, the US might see us as a foothold in Europe, what would be the cost?

As I proffer ideas for a domestic recovery in this book, I am aware that the global recovery will be fragile. The numerous sovereign problems that need remedying throughout Europe, together with the potential political and economic backlash of the German electorate, may pose quite serious problems for the EU in the not-too-distant future. As a nation, we must stay focused on those issues we can control while trying to influence those that are outside our remit but can affect us negatively.

We find ourselves in a strained partnership with Europe that needs massaging. There is a need for open dissent by both our European partners and ourselves. This openness will lead us to an acceptable solution that requires honesty and clarity in our discussions that may also demand a reappraisal of the EU and what its aspirations are and the price that needs to be paid. Will the political agenda outmuscle the economic one, leaving social discomfort and unrest on the sidelines of the field of progress? If there were only one or two countries within the union suffering a crisis then perhaps a solution would be more easily achieved. What, in effect, we are faced with is a lack of political leadership.

The major players in Europe that have diligently moved towards a United States of Europe have done so against relatively weak opposition. Political opposition due to the loss of economic sovereignty or the perception of being treated as a second- or third-tier member of this great union prevails in some quarters. But the political juggernaut will not be stopped in its quest for a unified Europe. If only a couple of the major players have the financial strength and political will to continue on the unification road then they must answer the challenge in terms of the costs.

Are the major decisions on the future of Europe made from an economic perspective or in the context of a strategic political long-term vision? Between the IMF, ECB, EU and Germany, are there sufficient resources and political ambition that will insist on taking a long-term view of the political status of Europe? Will the current situation and economic sovereign weaknesses force referenda to be taken on the question of the viability of a united Europe one more time? The electorate in Germany would be entitled to ask what the process of unification has cost them and if it will continue to do so. If the fulfillment of some economic and political vision creates nothing more than a loose confederation of dysfunctional members in a union, would Germany be better off withdrawing from the original vision and re-establishing itself as a strong central neighbour?

We have looked at the option of a two-tier euro, which I believe gets to the heart of resolving the economic difficulties of many of the ailing economies in Europe. Resolutions that put the interests of the investors and the markets before those who should be protected (the taxpayers) lead to suffering and social unrest. Many market observers want instant decisions, preferably wrapped in a couple of succinct sound bites that will help people understand more easily the need for swift, callous financial decisions. Those who influence the market and call for certain decisions to be taken with regard to the various troubled economies are unlikely to feel the consequences of their recommendations. Is it possible that we can call a halt to this continuous spiraling foreign debt that plagues not just Third World developing countries but major countries from the US to European states such as Spain, Greece and Ireland?

Whatever about the EU having a coherent plan, what about Ireland? What domestic steps could be entertained by Ireland to see us out of the current crisis? I feel I have identified many of the problems that the country is going to face over the coming years in terms of economics, banking and politics. I have tried to offer solutions to these problems, some straightforward and others far-reaching and complex. Whatever the decisions that are ultimately taken to resolve the problems we are faced with, we would be best served by a recovery plan and a clear vision of how the country should look after a couple of years of its implementation. We must establish a time frame within which we will consider our decisions and achieve our objectives, in line with the agreed financial protocols of Europe. I believe it would be a lot easier to take the economic and fiscal medicine to reduce our debt-to-GDP ratio and run a fiscal deficit of less than 3 per cent if we had a clear national plan. There would be nothing preventing us adjusting this plan if we are faced with further challenges domestically or from the international markets.

Recovery is likely to find its roots in those sectors of our economy where we have skills, interest and experience. Outside of an immediate injection of liquidity into the SME sector, plans should be put in place to foster and grow the technology, agriculture, financial services, media, and arts and entertainment sectors. Selective and considered investment into these sectors should produce positive returns and increase employment. Whatever national strategy plan is put in place, it would be folly not to find room for a modest revival of the construction industry. Our future is dependent on the export sector but we must avoid exporting our most valuable asset – our educated and ambitious youth.

Hopefully, whatever recovery plans are put in place, the Government and opposition will find it in their best interests to work together with a common objective. It is easy to argue that national mismanagement has placed us where we are today, but recriminations are not going to fix our problems; they are only going to add to them. There are a number of prerequisites to our recovery: the successful implementation of NAMA, a robust solution to the fiscal deficit, a substantial reduction in the number of people unemployed and strong measures to ensure the enormous public sector cost base is reduced.

If a fairytale ending to the current financial crisis is preferable then perhaps Hans Christian Andersen might take a better shot at writing this episode. Unfortunately, it is clear that no solutions can come without pain for every sector of our society. Another suggestion would be that the working week be increased to 5.5 days. Everyone in the country would be expected to increase their working week by some 10 per cent with no corresponding increase in wages or salary. The economic benefits of this action would be substantial. It would automatically increase production, reduce our cost base and very quickly get us on the road to recovery. However, the social implications would be substantial and the effects on quality of life would be harsh. While many will argue against increasing the working week on these grounds (and the EU might well have something to say about it too), it may be the single best way to demonstrate to ourselves and the rest of the world that we can take difficult decisions to protect and preserve our economy.

The Government has made it clear that its preferred method for recovery is to get the balance sheets of the banks cleansed and, through this, enable the banks to put more liquidity into the market. If the banks can manage to start putting liquidity into the market then one of the outcomes would be a controlled infusion of inflation into the system, in cooperation with guidance from the Central Bank. If this was managed in the right way we would see a steady increase in asset prices. For those who have been caught in the negative equity trap, this would be an avenue that would lead to an easing of the implied constraints therein. It should not happen overnight but be controlled over a three- to five-year period. This slow but perceptible increase in the price of assets would inject an air of hope and possibly renewed confidence into the economy. I cannot stress enough the need for control in the adoption of an inflation-driven recovery, for the consequences of uncontrolled inflation would be catastrophic.

If one of the key imperatives for the country is to reduce or erase the Government's liabilities, in turn achieving an improvement in the country's sovereign debt rating, then the sale of the cleansed banks to international investors must be a consideration. Perhaps getting the banks into a 'ready for sale' state should be considered in preparation for the possibility of new capital being injected into the banks or some major financial entities wishing to expand their European footprint into Ireland. However, giving up control of domestic banking would have negative effects, as the case of New Zealand demonstrates (discussed in Chapter 7). After twenty years New Zealand's four major banks remain in foreign ownership. Since the late 1980s, the income per capita in New Zealand has been close to the bottom quartile of the OECD (Organisation for Economic Co-operation and Development) ladder. Giving up control of our banks may carry too high a price. One other option on the banking horizon might be a once-off offer to customers to exchange retail deposit interest for warrants or shares in the banks, which would be a voluntary commitment.

The old banking model is broken and a new one needs to be developed. The two major banks have an uphill battle over the foreseeable future and, with the sale of some of their best-performing assets to strengthen their capital bases, large dependable cash flows will have been eliminated, leaving both institutions dependent upon the Irish market to repair their balance sheets. If both banks are now going to focus on Ireland then investors must wonder when they'll see capital growth, dividends and earnings per share return to acceptable levels. The future for these banks is about survival for the next few years. Due to the enormity of the problems in the commercial property sector there has been little focus on the potential losses of the SME sector by investment analysts. Mounting provisions will be required to offset the losses from the growth in insolvencies that were up 27 per cent on the 2009 figure for the first half of 2010; the year 2009 saw insolvencies increase by 80 per cent up on 2008.[50]

Looking over the financial landscape of Ireland as it appears today, I am saddened (others may simply be outraged) when I observe the destruction of the national financial services system.

Do the boards of the banks know what caused the downfall of their institutions and, if so, have steps been taken to avoid a recurrence? It is fair to say that the Irish banks were reckless in their credit management and, worse still, they were nowhere near prepared for the liquidity crisis that has occurred. I have no doubt as to the level of incompetency that has prevailed at management level within the banks.

The ongoing discussion on fairness and who in reality has to pay for the mistakes of executive bankers and politicians has led to the very political system being questioned. Have the political parties in the country adjusted to the changes in our society? Will the current crisis be the catalyst for political parties changing their policies for a new and better society? If the mainstream political parties in Ireland are seen to be failing the electorate, might this create a void into which more marginal, and perhaps less desirable, political parties will step? What are the alternatives to the current system? What, in effect, would be a 'better society'?

On a recent visit to Russia I learned about the changes that occurred in both the political and social environment over the past twenty years. *Perestroika* (restructuring) and *glasnost* (openness) were the two principal pillars of change. The centralised Soviet Union was dissolved in 1991 to make way for a loose confederation of states. The adoption of capitalism was painful in the early days. Private ownership was established through the passing of property that was once part of a collective to individual ownership. The history of callous decision making in Russia continued in the period of transition from socialism to capitalism, with the weak and poor paying the price for change. Only the strong would survive and this was the order of the day.[51]

Extraordinarily, today, the majority of Russians would acknowledge that almost all in their community are better off under the present system than they could remember being under the old Soviet system.[52] A once proud socialist state now competes at the highest levels of capitalism with its own model of private ownership and open markets. The local observer would comment that it might not have been the easiest of transitions but no major structural reform to a society comes easily. Are we as a nation evolving in the opposite direction to the Russians in our search for a fairer society? Before dismissing capitalism out of hand, perhaps those supporting socialism should take time out to experience a country where it is practised, or where it had been practised.

Any Irish political party would be tested today to come up with a political doctrine to reflect the values of the country and the mood that currently prevails. However, I believe that we need go no further than France to find a set of principles that would be, broadly speaking, acceptable to the Irish electorate: Liberté, Egalité, Fraternité. These principles had their origins in the French Revolution and were more formally adopted into French society at the end of the nineteenth century. But what does this motto represent that our Constitution doesn't?

Liberté – in France the general interpretation of Liberté consists of being able to do anything that does not harm others. Thus, the exercise of the natural rights of every man and woman has no bounds other than those that guarantee all other members of society the enjoyment of these same rights.[53]

Egalité – the law must be the same for all, whether it protects or punishes. All citizens should be equally eligible for high offices, public positions and employment according to their ability, virtues or talents, without other distinction.[54] This definition faces cronyism head-on and looks to a meritocracy as a preferred right.

Fraternité or brotherhood refers to moral obligations rather than rights, links rather than statutes, harmony rather than contract and community rather than individuality.[55]

As time passes and we begin to see an end to the crisis, we should reflect on what benefits we have taken out of this conundrum. If we simply address each problem as it arises without looking for positive outcomes for our society as a whole then we will do an injustice to ourselves through wasting an opportunity for change and progress.

Ireland needs a socio-political facelift that reflects a society that changed greatly in the face of economic blessings and has since experienced the jolt of an economic crisis. The Government has given to the electorate with one hand and are now forced to take back with the other, which is destroying trust and confidence, essential for a united approach to our recovery. Whatever risks need to be taken and managed, perhaps it would be opportune for all of us – Government, bankers, developers, public servants and private sector workers – to take on board the principles of Liberté, Egalité and Fraternité.

APPENDIX

Figure 1: Lending to the Private Sector and Deposits of Irish Banks as a Percentage of GNP, 1992 to 2009

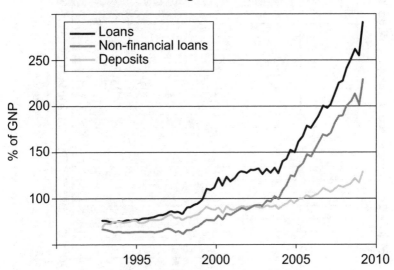

Source: Morgan Kelly, 'The Irish Credit Bubble', p. 7.

Appendix

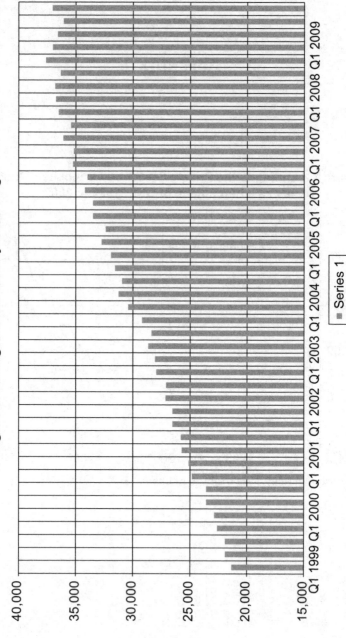

Figure 2: Average Irish Economy-Wide Wage

Series 1

Source: <http://www.rte.ie/business>; Economic and Social Research Institute (ESRI).

Table 1: Overview of Exposures to Portugal, Italy, Greece and Spain ('the PIGS'), December 2009

Adjusted Exposure (USD'bn)	Total EU Banks	Austria	Belgium	France	Germany	Ireland	Italy	Netherlands	Portugal	Spain	Sweden	Switzerland	UK
Greece	152.6	6.1	7.3	22.7	41.7	8.3	8.2	11.5	1.2	1.2	1.0	62.6	12.0
Portugal	144.2	2.6	8.6	33.7	42.6	5.6	6.7	11.8	0.0	0.4	0.5	3.6	24.5
Spain	582.4	6.5	30.2	155.9	102.6	29.2	28.4	116.7	15.6	0.0	5.6	13.2	60.8
Italy	582.6	13.4	45.4	152.7	103.2	45.4	0.0	75.4	5.3	35.1	3.5	20.7	73.5
Total	1461.7	30.6	100.7	305.1	440.0	86.5	43.4	214.5	22.3	39.8	10.5	100.1	170.9

Figures from the Bank for International Settlements (BIS), adjusted by Morgan Stanley International Research to include such claims as subsidiaries and other corporate loans.

GLOSSARY

AAA rating   The best-known scale for measuring debt quality is that used by Standard & Poor's which uses AAA for the highest rated debts and AA, A, BBB and so on for debt of descending credit quality.

Bank holding company   A company that controls one or more banks.

Basis point   A unit of measure used in finance to describe the percentage change in the value or rate of a financial instrument; it usually refers to changes in interest rates and bond yields.

Bond   A certificate of public or private debt that is bought and sold.

Bond rating   A rating company's evaluation of the probability that a particular bond issue will default.

Bull market   A financial market in which prices of securities are rising or expected to rise.

Capital ratio — The percentage of a bank's capital to its risk-weighted assets.

Collateralized debt obligation (CDO) — A type of structured asset-backed security, the value and payments of which are derived from a portfolio of fixed-income underlying assets.

Credit default swap (CDS) — A swap designed to transfer the credit exposure of fixed-income products between parties.

Debt-to-GDP ratio — This is commonly used to assess a government's finances by dividing government debt by GDP. Another way of using it is to divide total debt by GDP in order to establish a nation's finance as a whole.

Deleveraging — A process that is employed by financial institutions, businesses and governments to reduce the amount of financial leverage currently in place.

Derivatives — Financial products that derive their value from another commodity, security or other financial instrument. Also called 'swaps'.

Due diligence — An investigation of a potential investment, involving reasonable care to ensure all matters are in order before entering into the transaction.

Equity — The value of a business or property above any mortgage or liability.

Forward contract   A non-standardised agreement between two parties to buy or sell an asset at a certain future time at a price settled on today.

GDP   Gross domestic product: the total market values of goods and services produced within a nation's borders during a given period.

GNP   Gross national product: the total market values of goods and services produced by a nation within a given time period, plus income earned by its citizens abroad, minus income earned by foreigners in the country.

Hedge funds   Private investment partnerships open to institutions and individuals. These funds pursue returns through a number of alternative investment strategies, often not allowed in mutual funds or other funds.

Hedging   A strategy designed to reduce investment risk by buying or selling commodity futures as a protection against loss due to price fluctuation.

Investment bank   A financial institution that assists corporations and governments in raising capital by acting as the agent in the issuance of securities.

Leverage   The use of credit to enhance one's speculative capacity.

Liquidity   Assets that are easily convertible into cash.

Loan-to-deposit ratio   Ratio that assesses a bank's liquidity by dividing the bank's total loans by its total deposits.

Loan-to-value ratio   Assessment ratio that lenders use before approving a mortgage. The ratio considers the mortgage amount against the value of the property.

Market maker (jobber)   A broker-dealer company that accepts the risk of holding a certain number of shares of a particular security in order to facilitate trading in that security.

Marking to market   Settling or reconciling changes in the value of futures contracts (agreements to buy or sell assets) on a daily basis.

Private equity fund   A pooled investment vehicle used for making investments in various equity (and to a lesser extent debt) securities according to an investment strategy associated with private equity.

Retail bank   A financial institution that deals with consumers directly, rather than with corporations or other banks.

SME   Small and medium enterprise: business whose turnover and number of staff are below certain limits.

Structured invest-ment vehicle (SIV)   A type of structured credit product, popular until the crash of 2008.

Subprime debt   Debt that results from a particularly risky category of consumer loans; typically sold in a separate market from prime loans.

Swaps   See 'derivatives'.

TARP   Troubled Asset Relief Program: set up by the US Government to purchase assets and equity from financial institutions to strengthen its financial sector after the crisis of 2008.

Notes

1. Morgan Kelly (2009), 'The Irish Credit Bubble', University College Dublin (UCD) Centre for Economic Research Working Paper Series, UCD School of Economics.
2. Construction Industry Federation (CIF), internal paper.
3. From a personal interview.
4. Kevin Cashman (2003), 'Awakening Authenticity', *Executive Excellence*, May, available at <http://www.leaderpresence.com>, quoted in Gayle C. Avery (2006), *Leadership for Sustainable Futures: Achieving Success in a Competitive World*, Cheltenham: Edward Elgar Publishing Ltd.
5. Figures taken from <http://en.wikipedia.org/wiki/Great_Depression>.
6. *Ibid.*
7. *Ibid.*
8. Hank Paulson (2010), *On the Brink: Inside the Race to Stop the Collapse of the Global Financial System*, London: Headline Publishing Group.
9. Andrew Ross Sorkin (2009), *Too Big to Fail: Inside the Battle to Save Wall Street*, London: Allen Lane.
10. See note 8.
11. Paulson, *On the Brink*, pp. 439–440.

12. Entities are seen as 'too big to fail' if they are so essential to a macro-economy that their failure would be disastrous to the economy.

13. The eight financial institutions were Bear Stearns, IndyMac, Fannie Mae, Freddie Mac, Lehman Brothers, AIG, Washington Mutual and Wachovia.

14. <http://oxforddictionaries.com>.

15. <http://en.wikipedia.org/wiki/Cronyism>.

16. Transparency International Ireland (2010), 'Alternative to Silence: Whistleblower Protection in Ireland', p. 5.

17. *Report of the Company Law Review Group 2007*, available at <http://www.clrg.org>, p. 87.

18. See Deaglán de Bréadún, 'Support for Whistleblower Protection', *Irish Times*, 18 May 2010.

19. <http://www.fsa.gov.uk/Pages/Library/Communication/Speeches/2003/sp132.shtml>.

20. See <http://www.bis.org/publ/bcbs168.pdf>.

21. Figures from <http://www.rte.ie/business>.

22. <http://www.rte.ie/business>.

23. Joe Mulholland and Finbarr Bradley (2009), *Ireland's Economic Crisis – Time to Act* (Essays from the MacGill Summer School, 2009), Dublin: Carysfort Press.

24. Davy 'Weekly Book'.

25. My own observations of the market.

26. 'Opening Statement to the Joint Committee on Finance and the Public Service', available at <http://www.nama.ie/Publications>.

27. Figure from CIF, internal paper.

28. *Ibid.*

29. *Ibid.*
30. *Ibid.*
31. *Ibid.*
32. SIC (2010), information from press conference held on 12 April and an internal report.
33. From consultation with Peter Thodey.
34. Morgan Kelly, 'The Irish Credit Bubble', p. 7. See also Figure 1 in the Appendix.
35. Danske Bank (2008), 'Lessons from Swedish Bank Crisis Management', 30 September.
36. *Ibid.*
37. My own estimate.
38. <http://www.insolvencyjournal.ie>.
39. Shareholder's Register.
40. Wriston repeated this story at a lunch I was privileged to attend.
41. Figures from <http://en.wikipedia.org/wiki/2008%E2%80%932010_Latvian_financial_crisis>.
42. *Ibid.*
43. US Government Accountability Office (GAO) (2010), 'The Federal Government's Long-Term Fiscal Outlook January 2010 Update' (GAO-10-468SP), available at <http://www.gao.gov/new.items/d10468sp.pdf>, p. 1.
44. *Ibid.*, p. 6.
45. Niall Ferguson (2010), 'A Greek Crisis Is Coming to America', *Financial Times*, 10 February 2010.
46. 29 April 2010.
47. 'Years of Hardship Ahead', *Athens News*, issue number 13389, available at <http://www.athensnews.gr/articles>.

48. Morgan Stanley International Research.

49. *Ibid.*

50. <http://www.insolvencyjournal.ie>.

51. This was according to our guides in Russia.

52. *Ibid.*

53. *Declaration of the Rights of Man and of the Citizen*, 1789, Article 4.

54. *Ibid.*, Article 3.

55. <http://en.wikipedia.org>.

SOURCES

Avery, Gayle C. (2006), *Leadership for Sustainable Futures: Achieving Success in a Competitive World*, Cheltenham: Edward Elgar Publishing Ltd.

Barsch, Elga, Ineke, Jackie and Sheets, Andrew (2010), European Credit Strategy Monthly Call/Contagion Call Slides, Morgan Stanley International Research, 5 May, available at <http://www.scribd.com>.

Bradley, Finbarr and Kennelly, James J. (2008), *Capitalising on Culture, Competing on Difference: Innovation, Learning and a Sense of Place in a Globalising Ireland*, Dublin: Blackhall Publishing.

Danske Bank (2008), 'Lessons from Swedish Bank Crisis Management', 30 September.

Flannery, Michael J. (2009), 'Iceland's Failed Banks: A Post-Mortem', report prepared for the Icelandic Special Investigation Commission, November.

Heikensten, Lars (1998), 'Financial Crisis – Experiences from Sweden', seminar arranged by the Swedish Embassy, Seoul, Korea, 15 July 1998.

Sources

Kelly, Morgan (2009), 'The Irish Credit Bubble', University College Dublin (UCD) Centre for Economic Research Working Paper Series, UCD School of Economics.

Kroner, Niels (2009), *A Blueprint for Better Banking: Svenska Handelsbanken and a Proven Model for Post-Crash Banking*, Petersfield: Harriman House Publishing.

Lyons, Tom (2010), 'Financial Mandarins Don't Know Their Onions', *Sunday Times (Business)*, 5 May, p. 2.

Mulholland, Joe and Bradley, Finbarr (2009), *Ireland's Economic Crisis – Time to Act* (Essays from the MacGill Summer School, 2009), Dublin: Carysfort Press.

Paulson, Hank (2010), *On the Brink: Inside the Race to Stop the Collapse of the Global Financial System*, London: Headline Publishing Group.

Sorkin, Andrew Ross (2009), *Too Big to Fail: Inside the Battle to Save Wall Street*, London: Allen Lane.

Sprott, Eric and Franklin, David (2010), 'Weakness Begets Weakness: From Banks to Sovereigns to Banks', Sprott Asset Management.

Stelzer, Irwin, 'Road to Revival Disappears in a Fog of Confusion,' *Sunday Times (Business)*, 25 July, p. 4.

Stratfor (2010), 'The Making of a Greek Tragedy', 23 April, available at <http://www.stratfor.com>.

Transparency International Ireland (2010), 'Alternative to Silence: Whistleblower Protection in Ireland'.

INDEX